Praise for
Where Are the Armorbearers?

"I believe the key to the local church is the pastor. *Where Are the Armorbearers?* is an excellent resource for helping both pastors and congregations understand the need for armorbearers. Identifying and utilizing those whom God has called to give prayer and emotional support to church leaders is crucial to the success and even survival of the modern-day church leader."

— G. Dennis McGuire
General Overseer
Church of God International
Cleveland, Tennessee

"Bryan Cutshall has cut to the heart of the need for pastoral support. Having served as a pastor for more than 20 years, I greatly valued those in the church who prayed for me regularly, encouraged me often, and provided emotional support during times of crisis or discouragement. *Where Are the Armorbearers?* gives a Biblical and practical description of the role of the armorbearer. I recommend it to you heartily."

— Raymond F. Culpepper
First Assistant General Overseer
Church of God International
Cleveland, Tennessee

"*Where Are the Armorbearers?* speaks to a real need in our church today. Pastors are under attack almost daily and need the strength and support armorbearers can give. Bryan Cutshall, writing from a pastor's perspective, has experienced firsthand the value of having those in the church who prayed for him, supported him and encouraged him. This book is a must-read for church leaders, pastors and anyone called to provide support to those in leadership positions."

—Orville Hagan
Second Assistant General Overseer
Church of God International
Cleveland, Tennessee

"In a day of high stress levels and daily tensions, the key word is *relationships, relationships, relationships.* Recognizing this need, Pastor Bryan Cutshall makes a compelling case for the role of armorbearers to stand in the gap as irreplaceable gifts to help pastors maintain the delicate balance between confidence in personal abilities and the need to trust God for insight and strength to deal with weakness.

As a minister of 54 years and a pastor for 42 of those years, I wholeheartedly recommend *Where Are the Armorbearers?* as a book that not only focuses on the problem but also provides a strategic plan of action born from the combination of research and experience."

—Paul L. Walker, Ph.D.
3rd Assistant General Overseer
Church of God International
Cleveland, Tennessee

"*Where Are the Armorbearers?* is right on time and is a must-read, not just for pastors, but for laity as well. It will help clarify the calling and help identify the ones called. Bryan Cutshall has firsthand knowledge of the importance of an armorbearer and writes from this same perspective."

—Tim Hill
Secretary General
Church of God International
Cleveland, Tennessee

WHERE ARE THE ARMORBEARERS?

Bryan CUTSHALL

WHERE ARE THE ARMORBEARERS?

Strength and Support for Spiritual Leaders

Pathway PRESS

Book Editor: Wanda Griffith
Editorial Assistant: Tammy Hatfield
Copy Editors: Esther Metaxas
Aimee Norton

Library of Congress Catalog Card Number: 2005901035
ISBN: 1-59684-045-5
Copyright © 2005 by Pathway Press
Cleveland, Tennessee 37311
All Rights Reserved
Printed in the United States of America

Dedicated to the Current 25 Elders of Twin Rivers

THE HALL OF THE FAITHFUL

Hebrews 11 is commonly referred to as the "faith chapter." It is filled with men and women of the Bible who served excellently in their Kingdom call. I, too, could write a chapter of the faithful who have molded my life and ministry.

Now faith is the substance of things hoped for, the evidence of things not seen. For by it the elders obtained a good testimony (Hebrews 11:1).

By faith, Mike and Maggie have poured in love,
care and compliments while modeling worship and kindness.

❧

By faith, Matt and Phyllis have discipled,
counseled and served with the tenacity of warriors,
never even considering the cost of their cross.

❧

By faith, Bob and Georgette have organized, served,
loved and committed their lives to a call
of excellence to have a life in the Word.

❧

By faith, Dennis and Debbie have counseled,
opened their home and prayed the prayers of deliverance.

❧

By faith, John and Linda have fed the manna
from heaven and earth until God's people were full of love,
care, restoration and hope.

✦

By faith, Elmer and Mary have stood tall in the faith,
trained pastors on the mission field and changed the
lives of the youth who carry their legacy to never give up.

✦

By faith, Rabon and Mary have filled the air with song,
love, edible delicacies and spiritual morsels of truths,
and have anointed the heads of their leaders until their cups ran over.

✦

By faith, Bob and Millie have loved long,
visited faithfully and protected those in their care.

✦

By faith, George and Jean have mentored,
given out Prayer Bears, set a standard of excellence
in ministry and poured out wisdom like water.

✦

By faith, David and Mary have prayed, pulled down strongholds,
caused hell to tremble and lifted the hands of their leaders
in every battle as they fought at their side.

✦

By faith, Larry and Faye have served the army of God with honor,
dignity, a godly patriotism and the gift of humor.

✦

By faith, Gale and Sarah have beautified life
with ornate atmospheres while their greatest gift of beauty
was the example of their own lives.

✦

By faith, Phil and Donna have poured out love
like a fragrant oil that fills the room with the aroma of love,
joy, hugs and smiles.

❖

By faith, Randy and Vicky have given song,
service and sacrifice like it was as free as air.

❖

By faith, Jesse and Ellon have lived out Matthew 25
by taking in the stranger, feeding the hungry, visiting the lonely
and giving water to the thirsty. Their love knows no limit or price.

❖

By faith, Ron and Claudine have lifted the hands of men of God
and filled the atmosphere with angelic melodies
that penetrate the soul and change lives.

❖

By faith, Ralton and Waveney have preached and prophesied,
have encouraged and have built a network of bridges from
Twin Rivers to the city of St. Louis.

❖

By faith, Dave and Sue have filled rooms with memories of family,
faith and friendship, while turning special occasions into
life-changing moments.

❖

By faith, Larry and Marilyn have prayed
the prayers of faith while modeling
their commitment to their children, church and each other.

❖

By faith, Gerald and Sue have discipled,
served faithfully, and have spent a lifetime
serving their family and the body of Christ.

❖

By faith, Tony and Loretta have loved until it hurts,
and have made their home a haven for the weary
or anyone who needs to witness unconditional love in action.

✦

By faith, Roby and Tammy have birthed dreams,
and left a paper trail of hope, inspiration and education
to anyone who is willing to pick up that paper
and read their way to a better life in Christ.

✦

By faith, Howard and Jackie have given gifts
of administration and hospitality to
the world around them with a touch
of class that only they can provide.

✦

By faith, Carl and Pearl have served
with an Andrew spirit and, with a quiet and meek spirit,
they model faithfulness and servitude at its best.

✦

By faith, Charles and Pat have watered lives with
tears of joy, care and servitude,
and caused the garden of God to flourish with beauty.

Contents

FOREWORD

Bryan Cutshall, author of *Pilgrim's Promise: Getting Out of Egypt and Getting Egypt Out of Me* and *Conquering Canaan*, clearly demonstrates his understanding of the struggles, needs and enemies of the modern-day pastor or church leader in *Where Are the Armorbearers?* Cutshall does a masterful job of clearly and adequately defining the often- overlooked and seldom-appreciated role of the armorbearer to the pastor or leader. Using Biblical examples and ample Scriptural references, he paints an accurate portrait of the armorbearer's role, position, and relationship with his or her leader.

The book begins by laying the foundation for the need for armorbearers. Writing from personal experience and using the stories of others, Cutshall describes the challenges and battles that leaders must face and the need for someone to protect them from attacks and provide support and encouragement. He then articulates the Biblical description of an armorbearer and gives examples from the Bible, church history, and his personal experience as senior pastor at Twin Rivers Worship Center in St. Louis, Missouri. One of the most powerful chapters of the book deals with the difference between leaders having armorbearers or entourages. Cutshall includes a tribute to the armorbearers at his church and an armorbearer's pledge.

Having served in the role of administrative liaison to the general overseer of the Church of God for nearly 10 years, as I read the manuscript, I found myself readily identifying with the characteristics and principles that Cutshall delineates for the armorbearer. He opened my eyes to a new understanding of some of the challenges I have personally faced as I have transitioned through administrations and dealt with the issues of supporting the agenda of a new leader.

I wholeheartedly recommend this book for pastors and laypersons, leaders and their subordinates, and for anyone interested in cultivating this ministry of helps.

—Kenneth R. Bell
Administrative Liaison to the
General Overseer
Church of God International Offices
Cleveland, Tennessee

INTRODUCTION

S everal years ago I attended the funeral of a pastor friend of mine who died of cancer in his early 30s. There is no way to describe the questions I had about life, ministry, God, fairness or myself. It seemed like such a waste to me. Through the years I have come to accept the concept that because God is Alpha and Omega, first and last, the beginning and the end, He doesn't operate in the same time zones as we do.

I've learned to accept the fact that God sees every situation from the beginning to the end. That includes our lives and those around us who are a part of the circle of our lives. This event was a milestone of faith in my life where I chose to believe God even when I couldn't answer all the questions. It gave me a new sense of God's sovereignty.

But I find myself in an even more complex dilemma as I watch the slow death of many ministers, churches and warrior laymen. At least in the death of my friend, I was able to find closure. Yet, as I look upon the harvest fields of this world and see the number of ministers who are leaving the ministry, the number of clergy children who leave the faith, the number of clergy who lose their credentials for immorality, the number of laymen who leave the church, and the number of families dissolving, I meet grief on a whole new level. I am passionate about turning this cycle of pain around. I love the ministry and I love the ministers and laity who labor for God. I am convinced that if we can form an alliance between those serving and those being served, the cycle of nurture and care will replace the cycle of pain.

Where Are the Armorbearers? is more than a book. It is a plea filled with positive images of what I think church and servanthood is all about. My prayer is that pastors will use this material as a training tool for their leaders. One paradigm shift is all it takes to turn negative energy into positive energy. I am convinced that if we harness the energy and channel it in the right direction, the things that have been working against the church will start working to its advantage.

I love the kingdom of God. My greatest moments of joy are when I see my brothers and sisters win. Many times the Lord has placed me at the strategic moment of destiny where time and opportunity meet. I have been able to witness the reconciliation of trust and restoration of forgiveness. I am confident that if the armorbearers will take their appointed place in the Kingdom, we will become mightier and stronger than ever before. "One can chase a thousand, and two can put ten thousand to flight" (see Deuteronomy 32:30). I believe that second person in the equation is the armorbearer!

May the angel of the Lord go before you and make your journey prosperous.

David therefore departed from there and escaped to the cave of Adullam. And when his brothers and all his father's house heard it, they went down there to him. And everyone who was in distress, everyone who was in debt, and everyone who was discontented gathered to him. So he became captain over them. And there were about four hundred men with him (1 Samuel 22:1, 2).

1

The Choir of Cave Singers

Have you ever just wanted to run away, but didn't know where to go? A man showed up at my office one day from another state and said, "I just wanted to run away, but I didn't know where to go." I didn't really know him, other than meeting him a couple of times while I was speaking at a conference. I asked him, "Why here?" He replied, "I heard you preach a sermon years ago about a stricken shepherd and all I could think to do was get to the man who preached that sermon, in hopes that he would know what I needed to do."

He was leaving the ministry, his family, and all the investment God and others had placed in his life up to that point. After getting into a counseling program, we gave him love and friendship and eventually he was able to return to his ministry renewed from a state of desperation and burnout.

Can you image how David felt hiding in that cave? Saul had been throwing spears at him and plotting to kill him. In the midst of this attack, David learned there were many other desperate people in the world besides him. It must have been a large cave to house 400 men and their families who fled to this cave of refuge.

It is interesting to read about the exploits of David and his band of merry men, who were still capable of winning battles though ruined financially, steeped in depression and overwhelmed.

When you run to the cave, remember that even in your distress, you can still be productive. Just because one or two areas of your life shuts down doesn't mean you no longer have a place or purpose. Even the weary need a leader, and sometimes God uses one who has been broken and poured out to lead a group who is worn out, but still going.

> When you
> run to
> the cave,
> remember
> that even in
> your distress,
> you can still be
> productive

David's band of mighty men are a portrait of many churches. Some of these churches seem to be a gathering place for the weary and worn. God often appoints a leader over them who is a good spear dodger.

You don't have to be perfect to do the will of the Lord. As a matter of fact, we are all in the process of becoming what God wants us to be. Some go to the classroom to be perfected while others go to the blacksmith's shop to be forged in the fires of adversity. But whether God decides to use knowledge as power or turn pain into power, the end result is still a powerful leader who understands how to move people and get things done. I am convinced that the diploma from the school of "hard knocks" is just as valid as the one from the most prestigious learning institution.

SINGING CAVE SONGS

Some of the most beautiful worship in the world comes from those who are desperate for God.

- ♦ The woman with the issue of blood touched the hem of His garment, and we still tell her story.

- ♦ The woman with the alabaster box changed the atmosphere in a room because of her uninhibited, self-sacrificing praise.

- ♦ Habakkuk's song is one of the most beautiful songs of faith ever written, yet it came to him in a time of crisis (see Habakkuk 3).

- ♦ Paul and Silas' song in the jail was so powerful that God miraculously set every prisoner free and saved the jailer and his family, because two worn-out, broken-down preachers still had a song in the midst of their crisis.

After 40 years of desert living, burying three generations of loved ones, losing Moses, and living by faith, Joshua arrived at Jericho—the first city to be conquered in the Canaan land. Joshua tried to rally his worn-out troops to battle and indeed they were ready to go with him. But when they stood on the edge of their first battlefield, Joshua asked the angel, "What are our battle instructions?" The angel must have smiled as he said to Joshua, "God wants you to march around the city seven days, and on the seventh day He wants you to shout." Joshua must have wondered, *After all I have been through, can I still show up with a shout?*

Worship from hurting, broken and desperate people gets God's attention. Matthew 15 tells the story of a woman who cried out to get Jesus' attention. Her demon-possessed daughter needed His help. After several failed attempts of crying out to Jesus, she changed her method of approach. She decided to come worshiping. As she began to worship, He turned to her and spoke the words that freed her daughter from the demon that ruled her life. God loves cave songs.

David wrote some of his most beautiful music from that cave. One of the continuing themes of David's songs is "out of the depth." He used this phrase many times to describe the estate of his existence. He also used the word *refuge* over and over to describe God as a hiding place.

Listen to the words of one of David's cave songs and see if you can see the young man with his

harp singing this song beside a campfire in the
cave of refuge:

> *Have mercy on me, O Lord, for I am in trouble;*
> *My eye wastes away with grief,*
> *Yes, my soul and my body!*
> *For my life is spent with grief,*
> *And my years with sighing;*
> *My strength fails because of my iniquity,*
> *And my bones waste away.*
> *I am a reproach among all my enemies,*
> *But especially among my neighbors,*
> *And am repulsive to my acquaintances;*
> *Those who see me outside flee from me.*
> *I am forgotten like a dead man, out of mind;*
> *I am like a broken vessel.*
> *For I hear the slander of many;*
> *Fear is on every side;*
> *While they take counsel together against me,*
> *They scheme to take away my life.*
> *But as for me, I trust in You, O Lord;*
> *I say, "You are my God."*
> *My times are in Your hand;*
> *Deliver me from the hand of my enemies,*
> *And from those who persecute me. . . .*
> *You shall hide them in the secret place of Your*
> *   presence*
> *From the plots of man;*
> *You shall keep them secretly in a pavilion*
> *From the strife of tongues. . . .*
> *Be of good courage,*

And He shall strengthen your heart,
All you who hope in the Lord.

(Psalm 31:9-15, 20, 24)

THE CHOIR OF CAVE SINGERS

Many people who are reading this book belong to the choir of cave singers. Your paths have not been easy, but in the midst of your despair, remember that God loves cave songs. Don't forget to sing. There is no way to hear the choir on this side of heaven, for the members are scattered throughout all the earth. However, God hears their song. As each voice is raised toward heaven, it becomes a mass choir in the ears of the Almighty. Who is in this choir, you may ask? Their names will not be mentioned, but here is a description of their song:

God loves cave songs.

Verse 1

God hears the cries of . . .

Those who have preached to empty or cold pews.

Those who never got an "Amen."

Those who have propped themselves up to preach.

Those who beat out the paths so others could find their way.

Those who logged midnight hours.

Verse 2

God shows mercy to . . .

Those who had to hold back their own tears
so someone else could cry.

Those who have given more care than they
ever received.

Those who fill others' hands, but walk away
empty-handed.

Those who watched others take the credit for
their hard work and never said a word.

Those who bled so others could belong.

Verse 3

God gives blessings to . . .

Those who never owned a house.

Those who never saw the ocean.

Those who were limited by the traditions of
men.

Those who dreamed in silence.

Those whose courage outmatched their fears.

Verse 4

God answered the prayers of . . .

Those who lifted up weary hands.

Those who trimmed their own wicks and
kept their own flame.

Those who turned paths into trails and trails
into roads.

Those who had to cross the finish line limping.

Those who showed up, never gave up and are
one day going up for saying "Yes" to God.

Just like Jacob, you were transformed when you were left alone. Like Elijah, you pressed on in spite of fear and depression. Like Noah, you preached on, even when your message was rejected. Like Paul, you have mastered midnight praise. Like Jonah, you allowed your misfortune to serve as a lesson for other people's fortune. Like David, you sang your best songs in a cave.

You prayed hard, you loved hard, you cared hard; you gave again, you sang again, you preached again, you danced again; you dared to dream dreams, you flew the flag, you smiled despite your adversities.

You are the Choir of Cave Singers.

DISCUSSION QUESTIONS

1. What do you think the term *cave singer* means?

2. Discuss the text in 2 Samuel 22:1, 2.

3. Look up Habakkuk's song in chapter 3. Discuss his song.

4. Choose a psalm of David's that could be considered a cave song.

5. Pick out two or three types of people in the choir of cave singers and discuss the situations God may use to turn their pain into power.

Then He said to His disciples, "The harvest truly is plentiful, but the laborers are few. Therefore pray the Lord of the harvest to send out laborers into His harvest" (Matthew 9:37, 38).

2

Empty Pulpits

The harvest has never been the problem. There have always been plenty of sinners to fill every empty seat in every church. While we need to be concerned with the problem of empty pews, we have another emerging crisis on our hands that will have an even greater devastating effect on God's church. It's not an empty pew, but an empty pulpit. If there are no

> If there are no ministers, even those occupying the pews will eventually leave.

ministers, even those occupying the pews will eventually leave. Recent studies of why ministers are leaving the pulpit leave a searing truth in my mind.

- ⧫ 33% of pastors leave church due to conflict with the congregation (George Barna).

- ⧫ The average tenure of associate ministers and staff is less than two years.

- An estimated 25% of all pastors relocate every year.

- Most conflict in the church that causes a pastor to leave is due to fewer than eight people, regardless of the size of the church (John C. Maxwell).

- *Time* magazine reports that, in 1962, the Roman Catholic Church was turning out 42,000 new priests per year. In 2002, they turned out 4,000 and 60% of those were professed homosexuals.

- According to Lyle Schaller, we are closing 37 churches per day (13,505 per year). We are only planting 14 churches per day (5,110 per year). That is a net loss of 8,395 per year.

- 1,300 pastors each month are forcibly terminated without cause.

- A church that has fired its pastor has a 70% chance of doing the same to the following pastor. Each month, more than 1,200 pastors leave the ministry due to stress, church-related issues, family issues or burnout.

- 67% of pastors' wives say they are dissatisfied in their marriage.

- 75% of pastors spend less than one evening per week with their families.

- Clergy divorce has risen 65% in the last 20 years.

- 50% of seminary graduates leave the ministry after only five years.

- 70% of pastors say they don't have anyone they consider a personal friend.

- 71% of pastors say they're having financial problems.

Jane Rubietta, a pastor's wife and author of *How to Keep the Pastor You Love*, writes, "After a few years in ministry, I saw so many casualties across the country—broken pastors, church conflict, abandoned callings, too-brief stays at churches, and burnout—that I virtually called every denomination head in the mid-90s and asked, 'What are you doing for your pastors?'"

She goes on to say, "Caring for pastors goes beyond gifts and treats. If the pastor loses his love for God, he will certainly lose his ability to lead the church." In her book, she breaks down the largely unexamined myth of the superhuman pastor.[1]

OCCUPIED PULPITS WITH EMPTY WORDS

Job 21:34 says, "How then can you comfort me with empty words, since falsehood remains in your answers?" Long before the pulpit is vacant, the heart of the minister is vacant. Forced to rely on the relic of "preacher jargon" and cliches, the minister steps into his comfort zone each week to spread on another thin layer of the gospel. Empty words reveal an empty soul. Jesus said that from the abundance of the heart, the mouth speaks. The same is true about the lack of abundance. From the emptiness of the heart the mouth also speaks.

Warmed-over sermons with new titles reflect a loss of passion. Too many ministers are in the habit of preaching sermons instead of giving a message. There is a difference. A sermon consists of just enough gospel to make it legitimate, just enough illustration to make it interesting, and just enough outline to make it readable. A message, on the other hand, starts with "knee-ology," flows through theology and comes out hot, spicy and full of flavor. Sermons stir only the emotions, while messages change lives with timely, relevant, life-revealing, fresh-baked daily bread.

> Long before the pulpit is vacant, the heart of the minister is vacant.

There are many things God wants to accomplish that cannot be accomplished through a sermon. There are times when only a "word from the Lord" will get the job done. There are too many ministers and congregations who are hungry for a word from the Lord—a timely, fitly spoken and well-ordered word that loosens the bands and breaks the yokes that are holding back our lives and mission.

The passage from Job 21 indicates that "empty words" *cannot* and *will not* comfort, for there is falsehood in the underlying texture of the comments. Falsehood does not mean that it is a blatant and premeditated lie; it is simply an insincere attitude or intent. If you truly don't believe it, you can't really sell it.

> Often, before the sheep start leaving, they are already starving. Many of the sheep—even faithful ones—die a little each week from spiritual malnutrition.

Often, before the sheep start leaving, they are already starving. Many of the sheep—even faithful ones—die a little each week from spiritual malnutrition. They try to live on the dry, old morsels of spiritual food or on food too diluted to sustain them. The weakened shepherd no longer has the passion to properly prepare the spiritual table. Even those who live on spiritual bread and water often fall in the heat of the battle. Warriors must eat well in order to bring home the spoils of victory.

EXIT INTERVIEWS

This section represents interviews with different ministers who have left the ministry. While their stories have been printed by permission, their names have been changed to keep their families from further turmoil.

Interview #1—George

George is a college graduate with a degree in theology and psychology. He and his young bride dreamed of pastoring their first church all through college. She worked so that he could attend college full-time. Meanwhile, they had two children who were content to live in their small apartment that was filled with books, papers, a computer and the bare essentials. Life was focused: education now and ministry later.

Soon after George graduated, he was appointed to a church of about 150 people in the suburb of a large city. This was his dream come true. Drawing from all of his educational experience, he began to build what he thought was a great game plan. It wasn't long before George ran into a roadblock called "tradition." The congregation was comfortable with how things were. They simply wanted George to do what each of their other pastors did—maintain.

George's lack of experience began to show in how he dealt with the people. When he assumed his battle station called "pastoral authority," the battle of "tradition versus pastoral authority" was on. Soon a petition for his resignation surfaced. A secret meeting was called and with an overwhelming vote, George was voted out. With hopes dashed and dreams shattered, George and his young family decided that perhaps the ministry was not the place for them after all. This disillusioned couple began to struggle financially; their marriage began to be filled with turmoil and ended in divorce.

Today, George is remarried to an unbeliever and doesn't attend church. This came about three years after he lost his job and about two years after he was divorced. His ex-wife and children have found refuge in a church in a different denomination. They are still struggling—financially and emotionally.

Where were the armorbearers?

Interview #2—Tim and Jan

Tim and Jan appeared to be the perfect couple for ministry. He was as enthusiastic as a man could be about serving God. His zeal and passion made him the obvious choice for a staff role in a medium-sized church. At first, is seemed like a match made in heaven. The senior pastor was happy with their work and the church loved them dearly.

After a few months, the senior pastor began to get a little insecure about the wide reception of influence gained by young Tim. Soon he began questioning Tim's motives and decisions. The dagger was buried and the bleeding started. The wounds just got deeper and more infected as time passed. Piercing words of accusation and pain became the norm.

After contacting a few people in their denomination's leadership, Tim and Jan soon learned that everyone was sticking with the pastor. Lack of tenure, experience and relationships placed them at the mercy of a time-honored system of politics and power. Their zeal and innocence proved to be no match for such a powerful opponent. Soon they discovered they were left without an ally, representative or advocate. Their options were depleted, along with their security and support. Deeply wounded, they decided to leave the ministry altogether for fear of another breach of trust such as they had undergone. Tim's lament was the same as David's: "No man cared for my soul."

Where were the armorbearers?

Interview #3—Pastor Bob

Pastor Bob was a seasoned man of 57 years. He had built many buildings and had proven to be a choice administrator and church-builder. His track record was clean and concise. He was appointed to a new congregation, following a long-term minister who stayed in the church as a layperson. The first couple of years seemed to go well.

After the new board was elected, one of the board members, a relative of the former pastor, had a disagreement with Pastor Bob. One thing led to another, and soon the church was up in arms, with the former pastor leading the band against faithful Pastor Bob. The event came to a head at a conference where Pastor Bob stood as the target while one person after another took pot-shots at him.

One exaggerated story after another surfaced until his good name was marred with false assumptions and defamation of character. The disheartened seasoned warrior did not have the strength to start over, and slipped off quietly into the shadows. His early retirement and broken heart led him to an early grave.

Where were the armorbearers?

Interview #4—Gary and Charlotte

Gary and Charlotte left Bible school filled with ambition. Like most other young ministerial couples, they were going to change the world with their songs and words. With his new blue suit and her beautiful dress and never-ending charm, they set out on their assignment. As in many small churches, they were viewed more as the "caretakers" of the people rather than the ones God had sent to lead them to higher ground.

At first it was OK. Their zeal, youthfulness and desire to please God was enough for the demands placed on them. Charlotte didn't mind cleaning the church, and Gary didn't mind mowing the lawn, painting the walls and the other handyman chores. But soon, one demand turned into two and two turned into four. It wasn't long until their willingness to work caused them to enable the people they served to do nothing. The whole load was on the two of them. Burdened down, they began to feel worn out, tired and a bit angry. They were the ones who prayed . . . visited . . . did the manual labor . . . cared for the sick, the depressed, the dying, the lonely and anyone else in the community—including those who didn't attend their church.

In just a few months, they felt it taking a toll on their marriage, their attitudes and their health. No longer was there any time for each other or the plans they had made. It took them about three years in those trenches to decide it was not for them. With their hopes and dreams banished, this young couple left the ministry feeling burned out and mistreated.

This story did not have to end this way. First, Gary and Charlotte did not have enough training or experience to know that you must raise up leaders and delegate some of the responsibilities to them.

Second, no one in that congregation felt the call to be an armorbearer. One armorbearer could have saved their ministry. Gary and Charlotte both have good jobs today and are still married and serving God; however, the kingdom of God will never know the harvest that was assigned to their lives and the potential for success they would have had because there was no armorbearer.

DISCUSSION QUESTIONS

1. Read and discuss the "Empty Pulpit" statistics.

2. Discuss the concepts of occupied pulpits with empty words.

3. Read and discuss the exit interview of George.

4. Read and discuss the exit interview of Tim and Jan.

5. Read and discuss the exit interview of Pastor Bob.

6. Read and discuss the exit interview of Gary and Charlotte.

ENDNOTES

[1] Jane can be contacted at *www.abounding.org.*

Then He said to His disciples, "The harvest truly is plentiful, but the laborers are few. Therefore pray the Lord of the harvest to send out laborers into His harvest" (Matthew 9:37, 38).

Greater love has no one than this, than to lay down one's life for his friends. You are My friends if you do whatever I command you. No longer do I call you servants, for a servant does not know what his master is doing; but I have called you friends, for all things that I heard from My Father I have made known to you (John 15:13-15).

3

What Is an Armorbearer?

The word *armorbearer* appears 18 times in the *New King James Version* of the Bible. It comes from two Hebrew words: *nacah* (*naw-saw*), which means "to lift, bear up or carry," and *kalah* (*kaw-law*), which means "to end, complete or finish." Therefore, combined, *the definition of an armorbearer is one who lifts up and bears up the leader until the job is completed or finished.*

In many cases, the assignment cannot be completed because there is no armorbearer. The weary-handed warrior has no other option except to rest and regain strength while the troops wait on the sidelines for his recovery.

> Between the passes, by which Jonathan sought to go over to the Philistines' garrison, there was a sharp rock on one side and a sharp rock on the other side. And the name of one was Bozez, and the name of the other Seneh. The front of one faced northward opposite Michmash, and the other southward opposite Gibeah.

Then Jonathan said to the *young man who bore his armor*, "Come, let us go over to the garrison of these uncircumcised; it may be that the Lord will work for us. For nothing restrains the Lord from saving by many or by few."

So his *armorbearer* said to him, "Do all that is in your heart. Go then; here I am with you, according to your heart."

Then Jonathan said, "Very well, let us cross over to these men, and we will show ourselves to them. If they say thus to us, 'Wait until we come to you,' then we will stand still in our place and not go up to them. But if they say thus, 'Come up to us,' then we will go up. For the Lord has delivered them into our hand, and this will be a sign to us."

So both of them showed themselves to the garrison of the Philistines. And the Philistines said, "Look, the Hebrews are coming out of the holes where they have hidden." Then the men of the garrison called to Jonathan and his *armorbearer*, and said, "Come up to us, and we will show you something."

Jonathan said to his *armorbearer*, "Come up after me, for the Lord has delivered them into the hand of Israel." And Jonathan climbed up on his hands and knees with his *armorbearer* after him; and they fell before Jonathan. *And as he came after him, his armorbearer killed them.* That first slaughter which Jonathan and his *armorbearer* made was about twenty men within about half an acre of land.

And there was trembling in the camp, in the field, and among all the people. The garrison and the raiders also trembled; and the earth quaked, so that it was a very great trembling. Now the watchmen of Saul in Gibeah of Benjamin looked, and there was the multitude, melting away; and they went here and there. Then Saul said to the people who were with him, "Now call the roll and see who has gone from us." And when they had called the roll, surprisingly, Jonathan and his *armorbearer* were not there (1 Samuel 14:4-17).

THE HONOR OF THE ARMORBEARER

The honor of an armorbearer is dependent on one thing only: he must bring his officer back from the battle alive. Imagine a raging battle where the army is in need of true leadership in order to win.

The officer is their greatest hope for winning. His experience, wisdom and training can get them through . . . if he can get to the battle scene.

On the day of this great battle, there is one who wakes before the officer to begin making preparations for the battle. He is the armorbearer. The first duty of his day is to sharpen the sword of the officer. After that, he sharpens his own sword. Next, he shines the armor of his officer. It is important that the officer stands out from the rest of the army so they can see him clearly, for they look to him for direction.

After the armor is polished and ready, the armorbearer goes to the stables to bridle the fastest horses he can find to pull their chariot. He hitches the team and pulls up to the quarters of the officer to take him to the battle. The armorbearer drives the chariot while the officer rests. With his strength and focus set, nothing should deter him from focusing on the battle plan. The armorbearer also refreshes the officer with water and food. It is of utmost importance that the officer is ready and strong for the battle.

> The armorbearer's goal is bringing back his officer from the battle alive and unharmed.

Upon seeing the battle, the armorbearer stops the chariot and proceeds to strap on the armor of the officer. He hands him his freshly sharpened weapon. He then puts on his own armor and takes up his sword. The armorbearer listens for the instructions of the officer and guides the chariot to the strategic location of the command center. The officer has one goal in mind—winning the battle. The armorbearer's goal is bringing back his officer from the battle alive and unharmed. There will be other battles, and he must preserve the life of the one who can lead the army to victory. The honor of the officer is victory, but the honor of the armorbearer is the life of his officer.

> Wherever the officer goes in the battle, the armorbearer fights at his back.

If the enemy overtakes the chariot, the officer will take up arms and begin to fight as a foot soldier. The armorbearer will leave the chariot behind and take his place with the officer. His place is not at the officer's side or in front of him, but rather at his back. The officer is a skilled warrior and can fight well, but he needs someone to watch his back so the enemy does not sneak up on him unawares. Wherever the officer goes in the battle, the armorbearer fights at his back.

DUTIES OF AN ARMORBEARER

- Strengthens his officer

- Instinctively knows his officer's thoughts

- Feels a deep sense of respect for his officer

- Agrees with his officer and submits to the office of his leader

- Repels any kind of attack against his officer

- Rescues his officer from difficulties and hardships

- Keeps one eye on his officer and the other eye trained on the enemy

- Carries out every plan of his leader

- Watches while his officer sleeps and awakens him at the attacks of all foes

- Cares for his leader's belongings

- Brings acceleration and promotion to his officer's progress

- Reacts with total intolerance to any false accusations against his officer

- Refreshes his officer's journey by personally serving and waiting on him

- Aids his officer in spiritual combat

- Understands his assignment and also the assignment of his officer

BETWEEN THE PASSES

> Between the passes, by which Jonathan
> sought to go over to the Philistines' garrison,
> there was a sharp rock on one side and a
> sharp rock on the other side. And the name
> of one was Bozez, and the name of the other
> Seneh. The front of one faced northward
> opposite Michmash, and the other south-
> ward opposite Gibeah (vv. 14:4, 5).

It is not by mere coincidence that God lists the
names of these two stones. Their names reveal the
place where armorbearers are needed the most.
Bozez means "shining," and *Seneh* means "thorn."
Similarly, the Chinese word for *crisis* is made up of
two symbols. One symbol is tragedy and the other
is opportunity. What a true picture of a crisis. On
one side, you have an oppor-
tunity and on the other side
you have a tragedy.

It is between "shining" and
"thorn" that you need the
strength of another. On one
hand, you are wonderful,
while on the other, you can't
do anything right. Caught in
the middle of shining and thorn, you are pulled
between the opinions and labels of people.

> It is between
> "shining" and
> "thorn" that
> you need the
> strength of
> another.

This passageway is analogous to the route every
person must travel. The route is made up of suc-
cesses and failures: moments of glory (shining) and

moments of disappointment (thorns). This is the place where you are the most confused about yourself and the most vulnerable to the attacks of the enemy. You struggle to find the balance between knowing your strengths and sensing what you need to learn. You wrestle with the knowledge you possess and the power to build up; yet, you still seem to have the power to destroy.

You must not allow yourself to see only your strengths (shining), or you will become overly confident in your own abilities. At the same time, you must not become focused on your weaknesses, or you will be overcome with fear and low self-esteem. This passage is actually a good place to be because it is the balance between confidence in your gifts and the need to trust God for your weaknesses. It is the symmetry of reality. No one is good at everything and only the self-righteous get entangled in the web of self-deceit. It is good to see both your strengths and weaknesses in order to gather a staff to help compensate for your weaknesses.

> Breakthroughs are not victories. Neither can you live in the shadow of your last defeat, knowing delay is not denial.

This is where your armorbearer will become an irreplaceable gift in your life. The armorbearer stands in the gap with you between shining and thorn to keep you balanced. You cannot continue to live off the glory of your last breakthrough before the battle is over. Breakthroughs are not victories. Neither can you live in the shadow of your last defeat, knowing delay is not denial. This vulnerable place is a place of struggle where you must know yourself and keep your life in balance.

THE DECISION TO FIGHT

> Then Jonathan said to the young man who bore his armor, "Come, let us go over to the garrison of these uncircumcised; *it may be that the Lord will work for us.* For nothing restrains the Lord from saving by many or by few." So his armorbearer said to him, "Do all that is in your heart. Go then; here I am with you, according to your heart" (vv. 6, 7).

Jonathan admits that he does not know for sure what the outcome will be: "It may be that the Lord will work for us." As an armorbearer, you don't always know if the decision of your officer is the right one. Your commitment to bring your officer back from the battle is crucial at this point. There are times when your officer may use all the wisdom, knowledge and experience he has to make a tough call and still be wrong. Only one who is truly called to be an armorbearer can stand next to his bloodied officer and bleed with him. There will be other days for victory; just don't lose hope on the "thorny" days.

In 1999, our church decided to relocate. We had been trying to buy a shopping center and the arrangements looked promising. To purchase it, we needed to sell our existing building. I was surrounded with wise counsel as we embarked on this risky business. We accepted a contract and a down payment for our building and proceeded with our plans. Within weeks of our closing, the deal on the shopping center fell through. I had to stand before my congregation and tell them that we had to give up our facility without a place to go. All I could do was ask them to trust me. We had not acted hastily but, nevertheless, things did not turn out the way we had planned.

I will never forget the last Sunday in our old church. It was emotional for some, and unsettling for all. We planned to meet in a school that was about 10 miles away. Unforeseen to us, we continued to grow, even without a building. We outgrew that school gymnasium in about three months. Over the next two years, we moved 18 times before settling into the building we now call home. I do not consider this a defeat at all. We just had to stick together and follow God through our "see-nothing days."

It was my armorbearers who kept me encouraged during that trying time. It would seem natural for someone to wonder if I had truly heard from the Lord on that business deal. I still believe I acted in the best of wisdom, but with the understanding that God may have a different plan. As it turned out, we gained another 300 members during those two years, and God has used our "following-the-cloud" story to encourage thousands of weary pastors who were somewhere between the shining and the thorn.

Jonathan's armorbearer had to make the decision to stand by his officer even though there were risks involved. When an armorbearer truly feels called of the Lord to serve his officer, he does not keep his eye on the battle—he keeps his eye on the officer and the enemy. "So his armorbearer said to him, 'Do all that is in your heart. Go then; here I am with you, according to your heart'" (v. 7).

He understood his calling. He simply said, "My job is not to question you, it is simply to serve you. God didn't call me to advise you, just to keep you alive. I will follow you as you follow God. If we die today, it will be an honorable death. If we live, it will be a great victory."

I'VE GOT YOUR BACK

So both of them showed themselves to the garrison of the Philistines. And the Philistines said, "Look, the Hebrews are coming out of the holes where they have hidden." Then the men of the garrison called to Jonathan and his armorbearer, and said, "Come up to us, and we will show you something." Jonathan said to his armorbearer, *"Come up after me,* for the Lord has delivered them into the hand of Israel." And Jonathan climbed up on his hands and knees with *his armorbearer after him;* and they fell before Jonathan. *And as he came after him, his armorbearer killed them* (vv. 11-13).

God was going to deliver the Philistine army into the hands of two men. Great risks often bring great victories. Look at the order of this relationship. The officer goes in first, while the armorbearer covers his back. When you are on the same team and both of you are fulfilling your calling to the Lord, both of you win.

> There is a secret to advancing in God's kingdom: You can only lead as well as you can follow.

It doesn't matter who goes first, because one will not succeed without the strength of the other. There is a secret to advancing in God's kingdom: You can only lead as well as you can follow. The route to leadership is *followship*, not fellowship. It isn't about position, it is about obedience. Serving your officer is not about being his friend, it is about being his servant. It is your servitude that God will reward, not your fellowship.

Many people who want to lead do not want to serve. Many seek a title instead of a task. But God is choosing tomorrow's leaders from today's labor force.

*And as he came after him, his armorbearer killed them. He was fighting at the back of his officer, not at his side. Being an armorbearer is not about being a partner or even an assistant. It is about being behind the scenes as a protector. Because of the position of the armorbearer, no one could sneak up behind the officer. The armorbearer was saying to the officer, "Stay on the offense, and I will be your defense." He killed only those who came after Jonathan. As they came after the officer, the armorbearer came after them. A leader cannot fight the enemy while looking over his shoulder. It is the strategic position of the armorbearer that allows the officer to fight without looking back.

> A leader cannot fight the enemy while looking over his shoulder.

DISCUSSION QUESTIONS

1. Discuss the meaning of the word *armorbearer*.

2. Read and discuss the passage in 1 Samuel 14:4-17.

3. Discuss the honor of the armorbearer.

4. Discuss the duties of the armorbearer.

5. Discuss the Chinese symbols for *crisis*: tragedy and opportunity.

Women received their dead raised to life again. Others were tortured, not accepting deliverance, that they might obtain a better resurrection. Still others had trial of mockings and scourgings, yes, and of chains and imprisonment. They were stoned, they were sawn in two, were tempted, were slain with the sword. They wandered about in sheepskins and goatskins, being destitute, afflicted, tormented—of whom the world was not worthy. They wandered in deserts and mountains, in dens and caves of the earth (Hebrews 11:35-38).

4

Unsung Heroes

What is a hero? Technically, a *hero* is one who is admired for courage or outstanding achievement. Many courageous heros will never get a parade, a crown or a seat of honor on this earth. Yet, Heaven knows their names, and their seat of honor is still waiting on them. This is the group the Bible simply calls "others of whom this world is not worthy."

THE ARMORBEARER OF CHARLES FINNEY

One of the greatest evangelists who ever lived was Charles Finney. He preached in the 1820s. Nearly every place he went, he was met with opposition. Even though they ridiculed him and plotted against him, he pushed back the gates of hell in every city. It seemed as though Finney was unstoppable. His messages changed entire towns. He was usually met by a mob because word had spread that when Finney left, the town would be changed. Those who didn't want this revival often met him at the gates and with threats did their best to keep him out.

What they didn't know was that about three or four weeks before Finney arrived in a city, a man by the name of Father Daniel Nash went before him and prayed for hours each day over the town. Nash never attended the revival meetings, but he stayed in his hideout praying. Much of the public never knew the power behind Finney's preaching. In one town, the best he could find was a damp cellar, but this became his center for intercession. He would often try to find one or two people in every town to pray with him. There he trained them, and when he left, they would continue the prayer covering.

Finney wrote this in his journal:

> When I got to town to start the revival, a lady contacted me who ran a boarding house. She said, "Brother Finney, do you know a Father Nash? He and two other men have been in my boarding house for the last three days, but they haven't eaten a bite of food. I opened the door to peep in on them to see if they were all right and I saw them laying on their faces in a dark room groaning like sick men." She said, "I thought something awful must have happened to them. I was afraid and didn't know what to do. They have been

like this for three days. Can you come and check on them?"

Father Nash rarely was seen in public, especially during the revival, but on one occasion, a gang confronted Finney after a service and threatened him. Finney writes:

> Out of a dark shadow steps my good friend Nash. He said to this gang, "Now mark me, young men! God will break your ranks in less than one week, either by converting some of you or sending some of you to hell. He will do this as certainly as He is my God."

By the next Tuesday morning, the leader of the gang fell on his knees before Finney, repented of his sins and led his gang to the Lord.

In the winter of 1831, Father Nash died. In a cemetery in northern New York state, near the Canadian border, lies the body of Daniel Nash. If you find this dirt road, old neglected cemetery, and cheap tombstone, you will read, "Daniel Nash, Laborer with Finney, Mighty in Prayer, Nov. 17, 1775–Dec. 20, 1831."

Daniel Nash never made it to the elite of his time. Most people would have found this humble man unworthy of comment, but Daniel Nash was well-known in heaven and in hell. Nash did exploits for the King.

THE ARMORBEARER OF THE PROPHET ELIJAH

"But Jehoshaphat said, 'Is there no prophet of the Lord here, that we may inquire of the Lord by him?' So one of the servants of the king of Israel answered and said, 'Elisha the son of Shaphat is here, who poured water on the hands of Elijah'" (2 Kings 3:11).

How many people would settle for being known as "the man who poured water on the hands of Elijah?" When you are the armorbearer, you don't just see the leader when he is calling fire down from heaven, you also see him when he is struggling as a mere man. You see the ordinary side of the one you serve. Elisha was there when Elijah called fire out of heaven, but he was also in the cave when Elijah was suffering from depression. He was also on the hillside when King Ahab sent 50 men to bring Elijah in.

Elijah was so afraid he called fire down to kill them. Elisha saw his fear, his vulnerability, his struggle and his depression. But after he served him faithfully for almost 20 years, he said, "Before you go, I want a double portion of what you have. I know you are just a man, but I recognize you as the 'Voice of the Lord,' and it has been my privilege to pour water on your hands, cook your meals, carry your scrolls and refresh you on your journey."

The Bible records several occasions where Elijah tried to leave Elisha behind while he went on a journey, but Elisha said, "No. I go where you go. I will not leave your side." We can never flow in the anointing of Elisha until first we have learned to serve an Elijah.

There is only so much you can learn from a book or in a classroom. While that kind of knowledge is certainly profitable, it still lacks the smells, shadows, tastes and voices of personal experience. The best training field is still on-the-job training. If God calls you to be an armorbearer, He is offering you the benefits of the struggles, experiences and victories of another person's entire life. That is a book worth reading. It's not a book of pages and paper, but one written on the trails of life. The opportunity to learn from another man's experiences is priceless.

> If God calls you to be an armorbearer, He is offering you the benefits of the struggles, experiences and victories of another person's entire life.

There is no guarantee that an armorbearer is in training for leadership but, many times, this is the very route God uses to bring a person into greatness. Sometimes, God raises up armorbearers to continue the work of their officers and mentor. Perhaps this experience is necessary to truly know the heart and vision of their assignment from God. The Lord did not raise up one from the house of Elijah to succeed him, but he raised up his armorbearer as his successor.

The pattern of God raising up a righteous seed instead of a natural seed is found throughout the Bible. God did not raise up one of Moses' two sons—He raised up Joshua, his armorbearer. In Joshua 1:1, Joshua is called "Moses' minister" (KJV).

There is no guarantee that an armorbearer is in training for leadership but, many times, this is the very route God uses to bring a person into greatness.

God did not raise up Jonathan to be the king after his father, Saul, but He raised up Saul's armorbearer, David (see 1 Samuel 16:14-23). Even when Saul became jealous of David and sought to kill him, David, the faithful armorbearer, was true to the very end. He never laid a hand on his leader, King Saul.

God did not raise up one of Eli's sons as the priest in his place, but He raised up Eli's armorbearer, a boy by the name of Samuel, who became one of the greatest prophets in Israel. On many occasions, the anointing and success of the armorbearer exceeds that of the one he serves, but it is in his role of the servant that God chooses him, anoints him and establishes him.

THE REWARD OF THE ARMORBEARER

But Jehoshaphat said, "Is there no prophet of

the Lord here, that we may inquire of the Lord by him?" So one of the servants of the king of Israel answered and said, "Elisha the son of Shaphat is here, who poured water on the hands of Elijah." And Jehoshaphat said, "The word of the Lord is with him." So the king of Israel and Jehoshaphat and the king of Edom went down to him (2 Kings 3:11, 12).

Three kings were threatened with a battle that had the potential of crushing their kingdoms. They gathered their advisers, heads of state and military minds; yet all of them seemed uncertain as to the outcome of the battle. They decided to seek holy men to give them the final word—God's word for the battle. Each of them sought out the holy men of their kingdoms, only to find inconsistencies in their predictions. Finally, the king of Judah asked the question, "Is there no prophet of the Lord here?"

This was the moment when the highest title Elisha would ever receive was bestowed on him. The answer that came forth was not a title of an earned degree or pedigree, but one of reputation. The servant of the king said, "Elisha, the man who poured water on the hands of Elijah, is here." The three kings called for the "water-pourer."

This behind-the-scenes prophet had actually seen twice the miracles of his mentor as he carried on his mantle of power. He fulfilled his double-portion destiny, but when it came time to look him up, they called for the "water-pourer." He humbly accepted the title as one of high honor and dignity. He never corrected their assumption, nor tried to defend his reputation as a "real prophet." He could have told them about his double-portion miracles or the fact that he had broken Elijah's miracle record, but, instead, he accepted the title.

It is interesting to me that all three kings are direct descendants of Abraham. Technically, all are Jews, from the lines of Isaac and Ishmael. This conference of the three kings reminds me of a great day that lies ahead, when we, too, shall stand before the Holy Trinity of God and be rewarded for our labors on this earth. The Bible says that we will know as we are known. It also tells us that we will receive a new name, perhaps our true name.

In Hebrew, names have significant meanings. Perhaps our new name will be symbolic of our life on this earth. One may be called "Soulwinner," another "Worshiper" and yet another "Servant." I can see the scene with my spiritual eyes as God calls out the "Water-Pouring Club"—the Elishas who refreshed the spirits of holy men and women. Those who step forward will be among the eternal elite, for the first shall be last and the last shall be first. Christ's instructions to His disciples will be ever so clear as He said in Mark 9:35, "If anyone desires to be first, he shall be last of all and servant of all."

I can hear the voice from the throne as the crowns are placed on the head of each water-pourer: "Well done, good and faithful servant; you were faithful over a few things, I will make you ruler over many things. Enter into the joy of your Lord" (see Matthew 25:21).

TWIN RIVERS' ELISHA MINISTRY

At the church where I pastor, we have an Elders' Ministry that is truly amazing to observe. Each elder is given oversight of 50 to 100 people. The elders do almost all of the pastoral care for these people: they visit them, care for them, pray for them and answer their questions about life. As you can imagine, the role of an elder is very comprehensive and can be draining at times. In order to preserve our elders, each of them chooses a personal assistant we call his "Elisha." The Elisha serves for two years and then the elder chooses another Elisha. This ministry program has served to mentor many couples as spiritual leaders.

> The role of an elder is very comprehensive and can be draining at times. In order to preserve our elders, each of them chooses a personal assistant we call his "Elisha."

I will never forget when John Clark, a former

Elisha, came to me one evening and asked if he could have a ceremony of blessing for the elders at the close of our monthly elders' meeting. He explained his plan and I agreed. As 20 of our 22 elders at that time gathered at the close of the meeting, I invited them to follow me to the sanctuary.

We walked into a setting that I will never forget. The room was lit softly and worship music was playing in the background. There were several young men gathered who were either serving as an Elisha at that time or had served previously. These men had been praying for an hour and the atmosphere of the sanctuary was filled with the sweet aroma of prayer and praise. Many of the elders began to weep as we entered the room. The Elishas lined up on both sides of the aisle and, as the elders walked through the line of prayer, each man blessed them and prayed for them.

Next, the elders sat on the front rows as the Elishas set up a table filled with water basins and fragrant oils. As each elder approached the water basins, the Elishas who had served him poured water over his hands and spoke blessings over his life. Then the Elisha took the fragrant oil and anointed their elder's hands. There wasn't a dry eye in the house as we participated in the memorable experience.

The evening ended with all of us singing praise songs. Elder Haynes stepped forward to close the meeting by quoting the entire chapter of

1 Corinthians 13 from memory. The scene was electric and no one wanted to leave. I remember looking into the tear-filled eyes of an elder and saying, "All this and heaven too." We left that room so blessed and full of love!

DISCUSSION QUESTIONS

1. Who are your heroes? Discuss this question.

2. Read and discuss the story of Charles Finney's armorbearer.

3. Discuss the process of how God raised up Elisha to be Elijah's armorbearer.

4. Discuss the rewards of the armorbearers.

5. Have the class to practice a hand-washing ceremony.

Looking carefully lest anyone fall short of the grace of God; lest any root of bitterness springing up cause trouble, and by this many become defiled (Hebrews 12:15).

5

Who Will
Be the One?

One of the saddest creatures on earth is a bitter preacher. These two words are in such violent contrast, they should never be used together.

The root of bitterness is found in the original pain of disappointment, betrayal or criticism. If we do not allow the grace we have been given to extend to those who wound and hurt us, we open ourselves up to bitterness. When that root begins to grow in us, many people get defiled by our bitter words, suspicions, accusations and false assumptions.

MIGHTY ADVERSARIES

What is even sadder is that many of these murmuring warriors were once mighty warriors. Now, they fight with open wounds like blind and lame men on a brutal battlefield. Wandering from place to place . . . groping to find their way, they are at the mercy of anyone who will take the time to dress their wounds.

It is not easy to minister to a bitter person. Many

times, these wounded warriors hold grudges from the past—affixed on a timeframe that doesn't exist anymore. The more time that goes by, the more their memory gets distorted by the pain. The blood in their eyes begins to harden, and soon, their vision is impaired.

The lament of a bitter person usually goes something like this: "I used to be . . ." or "I could have been . . ." or "Look what they took from me." Many times, they blame the person who wounded them for their lack of success when, in fact, it was their bitterness that robbed them of their joy, peace, love and trust. They sabotaged their own success through their attitude and by focusing on their pain. Their constant babblings produced more pain for themselves and others. Paul writes to young pastor Timothy, telling him to "shun profane and idle babblings, for they will increase to more ungodliness and their message will spread like cancer" (see 2 Timothy 2:16, 17).

> While I believe it is never too late to repent or to forgive another person, we must also face the fact that we cannot undo all the damage that has been caused.

What do we do with a wounded warrior? Do we ignore him or do we dress his wounds? There is no pat answer to this question. It is a medical question. The first thing we have to assess is whether the infection can be contained or whether it has spread and taken over other vital organs. Has it created new problems? The original wound might have been small, but now it has caused spiritual gangrene to set up in the body. Does there need to be an amputation to keep the infection from spreading?

While I believe it is never too late to repent or to forgive another person, we must also face the fact that we cannot undo all the damage that has been caused. The truth is, we must catch the disease of bitterness in its early stage. That is why we need armorbearers. Thousands of soldiers could have been saved if someone had been there to apply a healing balm. Too many mighty warriors have fallen unnecessarily.

THE POWER OF ONE

Many warriors have been saved by the encouragement of one person. One person can do more than you realize. The Bible is replete with examples of what God can do with one person:

- David, a shepherd boy, turned Israel into a great nation.

- Samson fought an entire army of Philistines.

- Paul's footprints stretched across two-and-a-half continents and turned the Gentiles to

Christianity while writing more than half of the New Testament.

♦ John was taken to the isle of Patmos and showed the agenda of the world for future generations.

♦ The woman at the well brought revival to Samaria after meeting Jesus.

God has continued to use individuals to influence society:

♦ Martin Luther stood against the Roman Catholic Church and hid himself away to translate the Bible into the common language, because he was convinced that a Bible belonged in the hands of every individual.

♦ Thomas Jefferson wrote our Declaration of Independence.

♦ Henry Ford was convinced that men could ride instead of walk and, after three failed attempts and three bankruptcies, created the Ford Motor Company.

♦ Rosa Parks got on a bus and effected equal rights for all.

♦ Martin Luther King Jr. dreamed that all men were created equal and had the right to be free, and started a movement that would eventually break down the walls of racism.

It only takes one who says, "I believe" and will not compromise; it only takes one who refuses to give in to the naysayers and will stand his ground and be counted; it only takes one who will go the extra mile and refuse to blend into a world painted beige; it only takes one who will walk on, press in, take a leap of faith and see what others can't see. If one person can save a nation or a race or win a battle, then one person can save a church . . . if that one is an armorbearer.

ONE MAN NAMED DAVID

I have many people in my life who look out for my well-being. I am fortunate. I have a group of elders who constantly speak blessings over me. I have an inner circle of advisers I can talk to about anything. I have encouragers who speak into me and people who write me letters just to lift my hands. Unlike many preachers who serve alone, I do have close friends and even a best friend. My family and I have always lived hundreds of miles from our blood relatives, but God has richly filled our lives with people who have shared their holidays, attended my children's school events and concerts, and set places for us at their tables. Perhaps that is one of the reasons I am now performing wedding ceremonies for children I dedicated and baptized. That is one of the joys of a long-term pastorate.

My family and I feel loved by our church family and fulfilled by their love and celebration of our talents and gifts. To look at our large church now, it seems that pastoring this church should be easy and enjoyable. I have even had other preachers say to me, "I can do what you do." I am sure they could do what I do, but doing what I do and doing what I did to get here are two different things. What it took to get us to this stage is a different story. For the most part, we are in our due season, and have come through the hardest part of "paying our dues." We are now reaping what we plowed, tilled, sowed and cultivated. But don't be deceived by the crowds and multimillion-dollar complex. It wasn't always that way.

> It was in the embryo stages of my pastorate that God put a truck driver in my life by the name of David. Like David in the Bible, this man never backed down from a battle.

I came to St. Louis to pastor a small, struggling group of people who were only months away from closing their doors. They were on a fast decline of money and people when a 25-year-old pastor, his young bride and two small babies accepted the challenge and risk of praying down a "turn-around anointing."

It was in the embryo stages of my pastorate that God put a truck driver in my life by the name of David. Like David in the Bible, this man never backed down from a battle. He reminded me on many occasions that I couldn't quit because he wouldn't let me. He was the first man in my life to ever say to me, "God has given me the assigned task of making sure you complete your God-called assignment." I have to be honest; at first I didn't know how to take his direct approach and gruff way of dealing with me. He was as respectful as a man could be, but he didn't have time to waste words and dance around the issues. He quickly earned the right to call me off to the side and say, "What is going on with you? How long did you pray this week?" There were times on this journey that I thought he was my boot camp sergeant, but I soon learned he was the one that God assigned to bring me back from each battle alive.

Since that time, God has sent him some help (I must be a tough case), but he was the first and to this very day is still true to his calling to bring me back from the battle alive. The most amazing thing is that I never have to tell him when I am in a battle. He always knows without my saying a word, and he always knows exactly what the battle is about. It is almost like God gave him a secret window into my life to keep a watch over my soul. I can't get anything past him. I have ceased going to him with my issues—I never have to. All I have to do is be in a room with him for five minutes and he just knows. I can't even explain the relationship, but I do know he is the very reason I made it through many battles.

I will never forget an incident that happened many years ago when we were on a missions trip together. While building a church in El Salvador, we were in the dry season and ran out of water on the work site. The team was discouraged. There was no way to mix the concrete without water. David saw the stress I was under and came over to the crowd gathered around me and said, "Do you mean all we are worried about is water?" He lifted his head heavenward and simply asked God to send water.

It was nearing the end of the day, so we all went back to the campground where we were staying. In the middle of the night, we heard the chariots of God rolling into the camp as the clouds burst forth in rain for about 30 minutes. The national overseer of El Salvador told us that he had lived in that country for more than 40 years and it was the first time he had ever seen rain in that particular month. The rain hadn't lasted long, but the next day when we arrived at our work site, all of our water barrels were running over.

On another occasion, I saw him step in front of a swarm of hornets that he thought were going to sting me. He spoke a word of death over them and, to my amazement, the entire swarm died instantly. He never told that story to anyone that I know of, but I will never forget it as long as I live. One man can make a difference.

THE LEGACY OF AN ARMORBEARER

David is now 77 years old and still just as strong in his faith as I have ever seen him. Recently, he walked through the rain forest of Central America with me and a few other missionaries. We took canoes through the jungles to minister to the Miskito Indians.

David's son-in-law, Don, became my Sunday armorbearer. Don is a natural servant and has a heart of gold. I certainly didn't ask Don to do all the things he does, but he is determined that on Sundays, I will be able to walk to the pulpit fresh. He meets me at the door when I arrive and parks my car. He brings in my briefcase or anything I need to carry to my office. He even asks me each Sunday if he can shine my shoes. The spirit of David rests on the spirit of Don.

Only eternity will reveal the rewards of this family and their legacy of preserving my family's ministry. They have saved my life more times than I can count—by refreshing me, keeping me from getting bogged down in preservice details, making sure I get to where I need to be in the building, getting me coffee in between the services, and constantly pouring prayer and encouragement into my life.

WHO WILL BE THE ONE?

There are many pulpits that would be filled with power today if there was just one person who would take on the role of an armorbearer. So many pastors wear themselves out, unlocking doors, turning on lights, greeting the people as they come in the building, teaching a class, preaching a sermon, praying for the sick and needy, encouraging people, counseling, visiting, doing church business, hospital calls, weddings, funerals, and some are even required to do the cleaning and maintenance of the building and church grounds. Anyone can paint a wall or cut grass, but only the anointed can cast out demons, pray the prayer of faith and set the captives free. We don't need our men and women of God stressed out. We have to live in victory on what they are teaching and preaching. We need someone who has time to walk and talk with God—someone who can walk in the anointing and take authority over sickness, depression and oppressive spirits. What many churches are expecting is impossible to deliver. They want a shepherd, maintenance man and holy man.

The most important role is that of a holy man.

> There are many pulpits that would be filled with power today if there was just one person who would take on the role of an armorbearer.

We need men and women of power in our pulpits. We need people who walk in the room and their very presence brings a calm and peace. We need to free up our ministers so they can minister. The reason deacons were appointed in Acts 6 was to keep the ministers from waiting on tables. The word *deacon* means "table waiter."

> We need to free up our ministers so they can minister.

They were appointed to take care of the business of the church so the ministers could minister. It was the appointment of deacons that caused the church to grow. The Bible says that souls were added to them daily, when the deacons got in their rightful place and the ministers were freed up to do God's work. It only takes one to make the difference. Who will be the one?

DISCUSSION QUESTIONS

1. Discuss possible scenarios where warriors might become wounded warriors.

2. Discuss the power of one. What can one person do that will make a difference?

3. Read and discuss the section on "Who Will Be the One?"

4. Ask each person to name his or her favorite Bible character and discuss how that one life made a difference.

5. Ask the group members to discuss how one person has affected or changed their lives.

Let us not give up meeting together, as some are in the habit of doing, but let us encourage one another—and all the more as you see the Day approaching (Hebrews 10:25, *NIV*).

6

The Ministry of Encouragement

When God created the world, He didn't make it with His hands; He spoke it into existence. He simply said, "Let there be . . ." and it was so. Many people do not realize that He put that same ability inside His children. No, we can't speak a tree or an ocean into existence like He did, but we do create the world around us with our words. The power of life and death is in the tongue, and each day of our life we are speaking either life or death into our loved ones, friends, coworkers or acquaintances.

YOU CREATE THE WORLD AROUND YOU WITH YOUR WORDS

Wars have been started over words. Lives have been saved over words. Presidents are elected because of words. We can never underestimate the power of saying what we are thinking to a person who has value in our life. I wasn't sure if I wanted to include letters that I have received through the years, but I felt it might help an armorbearer to see the need to encourage their man or woman of God in this way. These are only a few of hundreds of letters I have received through the years. In addition to the letters are also cards, e-mails and gifts from time to time.

We can never underestimate the power of saying what we are think-ing to a person who has value in our life.

My favorite file is one titled "Drawings From Children." I have over 200 drawings children in my church have given to me after the services. Many of them bring their drawing pads and draw a picture that describes what I am preaching. It is their own way of taking notes. This file is one of my true treasures in life. From time to time, I get out the file and look through the pictures again, just because it makes me smile. Especially on a rainy day, when the office is slow, I close my door, get a cup of coffee, and sit back in my chair and look through this file. It reminds me that what I do is important. Even though I have to wait years to see some of my harvest in ministry, this file reminds me that the seed is in the ground.

This chapter is very personal to me. It is my way of sharing some of my choice treasures: a few letters and pictures.

Dear Pastor,

I just wanted to tell you what a blessing the entire early service was to me last Sunday morning. I am sure the scripture you shared (Matthew 11:28-30) blessed many there, but it was a direct encouragement to me.

I find that I often need to be reminded that His yoke is easy and His burden is light. I got a mental picture of a large ocean wave. I can choose to ride with that wave and have an exciting, but peaceful ride, or I can choose to fight the wave, gulp water and face possible disaster. I was reminded that I often have preconceived ideas of how God should operate in my life. Just because He isn't using me as He has always done does not mean that He is not using me or that He is not pleased. I have been straining at the yoke and making my burden greater. I remember, very clearly, your words that the message does not change, yet, the method may. Also, I remember that lopsided yoke illustration from your sermon years ago. Thank you for allowing the Lord to use you to remind me to get back in step!

I was so encouraged with the conversation you had with the Lord as He told you that you may not carry the gospel to the nations, but you would train those who would. Just think of how many lives you touch in doing that! This helps me to accept where I am and what He is doing with me. Thank you for being so open.

The Lord had taken me to Isaiah 58 shortly before we returned to this area. Many of the thoughts you shared confirmed to us what the Lord has directed.

We appreciate you so much. You never cease to have a current word for us all. With much thankfulness and appreciation for you.

—Mike

Dear Pastor,

I feel the Lord gave me this verse to share with you: "You are the most excellent of men and your lips have been anointed with grace, since God has blessed you forever" (Psalm 45:2, *NIV*). I am not sure why I was to share this with you as I know how blessed and humble you feel in the way He keeps using you. Maybe it is just to be a confirmation of His love and blessings for you.

Our church family is so blessed to have you as our shepherd. I will continue to pray for you and your faithfulness.

—Edith

Dear Pastor,

I am so excited about what God is doing! I cannot thank Him enough for the changes in our lives!

We come every week to worship Him and hear a fresh word from the Lord. It is always fresh; always new. He addresses the issues we are dealing with, or He is preparing us for what is to come. He is doing so much in us and for many other people that we talk to. He is preparing His people.

God has touched many lives through the obedience of you and Faith. It is through the worship and the washing of the Word. It is then that people are delivered from sin and set free. Freedom comes with applying God's Word.

He has proved Himself many times. We cannot stop the application. Thank you for listening to God and saying what needs to be said.

Keep looking up!

—Karen

Dear Pastor Bryan and Faith,

We wanted to tell you both how much we enjoyed the early service. The music was wonderful! The anointing was obvious and the Spirit just flowed. Faith, what a blessing it was for us! We both felt that there was a real intimacy among those who were gathered there. Thank you for giving so unconditionally of yourself.

Pastor, I cannot tell you how I have utilized your message during my prayer time this week. Prayer is and always has been an important priority to me. The plan that you presented to us has only enhanced that time for me. I see the Lord's Prayer in a whole new perspective now and it means even more than it did before!

Knowing that you are doing two totally different services makes it difficult for us to leave after the early service, but we realize that staying may defeat the purpose in having the two services "to spread the masses," so there is ample room for all.

Thank you both for your efforts. We pray that God will strengthen you to accomplish His purpose and rest you physically, emotionally and spiritually over the time to come. We continue to "hold up your arms" as you obediently follow His leading. How thankful we are to be under your leadership!

—Mike and Mary

THE BACKBONE OF MINISTRY

The Ministry of Encouragement at Twin Rivers has been the backbone of many ministries, yet this role often goes unrecognized. An encourager is usually a person who works behind the scenes and is seldom recognized publicly. The truth is that most of them prefer to do their work in secret and would rather not be recognized. At Twin Rivers, where I pastor, we have a ministry called the Ministry of Encouragement. There are over 150 people involved in this ministry. Each encourager is given five families in the church to encourage. Their job is to call them once a month and pray with them on the phone. In addition, they send them cards and letters. We also ask them to look them up at church on Sunday and greet them with a handshake or a hug. This continual contact gives each family in the church a personal minister of encouragement. Each month during their prayer, if the encourager feels the individual or family needs additional follow-up, they will notify their elder and the elder will take the matter from that point. It is truly an amazing ministry and keeps people from falling through the cracks in a large congregation.

DISCUSSION QUESTIONS

1. Discuss the ministry of encouragement.

2. Ask the members of the group to write a let-ter of encouragement to someone.

3. Discuss how an encourager changed the individual lives of the class members.

4. Ask the group to write a job description for a minister of encouragement, focusing on the character traits of an encourager.

You know that the rulers of the Gentiles lord it over them, and those who are great exercise authority over them. Yet it shall not be so among you; but whoever desires to become great among you, let him be your servant. And whoever desires to be first among you, let him be your slave—just as the Son of Man did not come to be served, but to serve, and to give His life a ransom for many (Matthew 20:25-28).

7

Armorbearers or Entourages

Here he comes: A prizefighter enters the arena filled with cheering fans. The moment is his. Cameras are flashing, newspaper reporters are writing, and the air is charged with momentum or, as some call it, "Big Mo." The hero is hidden. You can only catch a glimpse of him from time to time because he is surrounded by an entourage. Oh yes, his people—the people who keep him from the crowd, the people who serve as a human barrier between him and those who just want to touch him. Yes, his people—the ones who make sure no one gets too close. They protect him by pushing people away and get him to the stage so he can perform for the crowd.

This scene could accurately describe the entrance of many dignitaries, politicians, actors, performers or athletes but, according to the patterns of the Bible, should never resemble the entrance of a man or woman of God.

THE KINGDOM ELITE

In the world we live in today, more and more

ministers are starting to resemble the entrance of the prizefighter. I know that some ministries get so large that the crowd can pull and tug on them, but they must be careful to remember the examples set for us by the Biblical holy men and women and, most important, the ministry of the Lord himself.

Each time the disciples reacted to the crowd like an entourage, Jesus rebuked them. We can't forget the lesson of Matthew 19:13-15:

> Then little children were brought to Him that He might put His hands on them and pray, but the disciples rebuked them. But Jesus said, "Let the little children come to Me, and do not forbid them; for of such is the kingdom of heaven." And He laid His hands on them and departed from there.

THE MODEL OF THE MINISTRY OF JESUS

Jesus had 12 men at His side, but they did much more than merely protect Him from the crowd, even though the Bible mentions often that the multitude pressed Him. We see the disciples passing out bread and fish and then cleaning up the fragments, among many other acts of service.

Who were these 12 men and what did they do? According to their previous occupations, they ranged from fishermen and tax collectors to riotous political activists. Some were brothers, but almost all were strangers. One thing is for sure, from a business angle—they looked like a ragtag group randomly gathered with little hope of ever working together to accomplish anything. Yet, this is the group Christ chose to be the first ambassadors (apostles) of the church.

The apostolic role was an administrative role. They were literally supposed to go from city to city and establish order in the newly formed churches. But from all appearances, they did well to get through a meal together without an argument or debate. There was impulsive Peter, who acted in haste. We could never forget the Sons of Thunder, James and John, who were vying for position. Then there is doubting Thomas, who was sure to throw a damper on a dinner party. And let's not forget greedy Judas, who carried the money bag for Jesus' ministry.

> The apostolic role was an administrative role. They were literally supposed to go from city to city and establish order in the newly formed churches.

But in spite of the incredible odds against making anything out of this group, the Master Teacher began to pour life into them through His words. In addition, He knew that the deposit of the Holy Spirit into their lives would change everything.

In the meantime, what did these Twelve do

during their three-year training program? Most of their jobs had to do with serving Christ, each other and the crowd. On several occasions, we see the disciples praying for the crowd as Jesus ministered to them. Other times, they were preparing rooms for supper, fetching donkeys and retrieving coins from the mouths of fish. They waited tables, washed feet, and even did a little cooking and grocery shopping. As a part of the ministry of Christ, they prepared the way for ministry and assisted in carrying out the plan for that day. Even to the untrained eye, the role they performed resembled the role of armorbearers far more than a superstar's entourage.

NEVER GET TOO BIG TO SERVE

Those who lead must also serve. Servitude is the road to greatness. People who develop great minds but lose heart eventually become useless in Kingdom work. The people of the Kingdom do not do what they do because of intellectual decisions. If you merely decide to enter Kingdom work, you can decide to quit, and there will be days you will be tempted to do just that. However, if you were called to the work, you don't have the option to stop until you first check in with the same voice that called you in the first place.

For this reason, the hearts of God's leaders must be developed along with their skills and wills. If leaders ever lose heart and get to the point that they forget the Kingdom elite are servants, they cease to build His kingdom and start to build their own.

I believe in giving honor to whom honor is due. I do believe in serving holy men and women, but I also believe the ones being served should never get too comfortable being served. It is easy to get to the point that service is demanded, or even required, before ministry is "performed." That should never be the case. The thronging-multitude moments can easily make one feel so exalted that he can lose sight of what the Lord saw in him to begin with.

> If leaders ever lose heart and get to the point that they forget the Kingdom elite are servants, they cease to build His kingdom and start to build their own.

NEVER FORGET YOUR "JOURNEY" TO GREATNESS

We must never forget where we were when He picked us up. We must never forget our moments of desperation, when our assignment was bigger than our skill. We must never forget our days of loneliness, when He took us to a wilderness to teach us so we wouldn't be distracted from the lesson. We must never forget the

> We must never forget our moments of desperation, when our assignment was bigger than our skill.

small beginnings, the people who invested in us early, the encouragers who believed in us when we couldn't even believe in ourselves—never forget the people who mentored us and saw gifts of greatness in us when we couldn't even see how to get through the week. We can't let the pressing crowd fool us into thinking they are the ones who made us important enough to be celebrated. The crowd loves what we give to them, but the armorbearer loves us even in our struggles.

Our journey is where God trained us, taught us and built our character. It was in the back field that God chose David to be king. Jesus chose His disciples when many of them were either "down and out" or still in their sin. He chooses the foolish things of the world to confound the wise for a reason. God wants the ordinary to become the extraordinary to display His glory. But we must never forget how the Lord's Prayer ends, "For Thine is the kingdom, the power and the glory, forever."

It is always His kingdom, His power and His glory—regardless of our success. Our journey is the insurance that when we rise to the top, we give Him the glory for it. Without a struggle, we would get the idea it was only our gift and talent that caused us to rise. The struggle keeps us humble and dependent on God.

SERVERS OR STRUTTERS?

We must never get arrogant in our anointing, for pride comes just before a fall. We need to confess that even great men and women get tempted. Even the giants in the Kingdom, the mighty men, have a thorn in the flesh that buffets them. We are not above a struggle or a moment of weakness; therefore, we cannot turn our armorbearers into entourages. They must remain

> Our journey is the insurance that when we rise to the top, we give Him the glory for it.

the warriors at our side who help us fight the real battles—not strutters who sashay us through the crowd to make us look prominent and important.

The key to Kingdom leadership is still servitude. You never achieve a level of accomplishment where you can no longer serve. Perhaps the greatest reason the disciples served instead of strutted is because of what took place behind the scenes in the ministry of Christ. Fortunately for us, the Bible records Christ's intimate moments with His disciples. One scene in John 13 is a personal moment Christ had with them just before the

Crucifixion. In this scene, He leaves them with a powerful example of how to be a leader in the kingdom of God.

> So when He had washed their feet, taken His garments, and sat down again, He said to them, "Do you know what I have done to you? You call Me Teacher and Lord, and you say well, for so I am. If I then, your Lord and Teacher, have washed your feet, you also ought to wash one another's feet. For I have given you an example, that you should do as I have done to you. Most assuredly, I say to you, a servant is not greater than his master; nor is he who is sent greater than he who sent him" (vv. 12-16).

There are so many things Christ could have done or said to leave a lasting impression on the 12 men He chose to lead the church, but nothing could have had more impact than the day He girded Himself with a towel and washed their feet. Peter was so humbled by it that at first, he refused. I would have loved to have seen the reaction of these men as the Lord showed them His servant's heart.

You never achieve a level of accomplishment where you can no longer serve.

If we truly believe that leadership begins at the top, then leaders who are being served must ask themselves if they are also washing the feet of those who lift their load. When it comes down to the bottom line, the real difference is whether they have armorbearers or an entourage mentality. Leaders who are servants will most likely be surrounded by armorbearers. Leaders who are more into being served than serving others have an entourage.

DISCUSSION QUESTIONS

1. Discuss the concept of the "minister's entourage."

2. Who do you think are the Kingdom elite? Discuss this question.

3. Discuss the model of Jesus' ministry.

4. Discuss John 13:12-16.

5. Discuss the concept of servers or strutters.

Then all the trees said to the bramble, "You come and reign over us!" And the bramble said to the trees, "If in truth you anoint me as king over you, then come and take shelter in my shade; but if not, let fire come out of the bramble and devour the cedars of Lebanon!" (Judges 9:14, 15).

8

The Leadership Crisis

Can you imagine the national fallout of empty pulpits? When you consider the crisis of empty pulpits in America, you can see a trend developing that will affect the next generations more severely than the present generation. As we continue to close down churches in America, the casino, pornography and drug industries are growing and thriving. There is hope when national reports reflect that the 2004 Presidential Election was turned on the moral and ethical issues of the conservative-evangelical Christian votes.

Unless we begin to produce quality church planters and continue to raise up leaders who can lead the Kingdom work at the same level our forefathers did, we will find ourselves with a leaderless army.

"A LEADERLESS ARMY CAN'T MARCH"

New faces and voices must come to the forefront

in order for us to remain effective. History and tradition can only carry us so far. Each generation must experience a revival. Today's up-and-coming leaders seem too preoccupied with income, impressive numbers and popularity.

Our forefathers filled their days with prayer—seeking God's will for His kingdom. We cannot return to the methods of the past, but we must return to the message of the past. Unless we turn this crisis around, we will continue to die a slow death. One day we will be walking through a cemetery of saints, or a battlefield of dead soldiers, and not know how it happened.

If you see an enemy coming, you can create a strategy, plan the attack, and win the victory. But this subtle enemy of decline is like a couple who have been married for so many years they barely notice when their love, fun and passion walk out the door. They just continue to live in the day-to-day routine of life, until one day they realize that both of them are dead on the inside. The marriage is nothing more than a boring routine of mundane duties and responsibilities. Out of convenience and tiredness, they never know the power of passion.

We cannot allow the church to go down the road of slow death in America. It has already happened in Germany and in much of Europe. Nations that were once 70 percent Christian are now 2-3 percent Christian.

While we look across the nation at many megachurch ministries that are flourishing and growing, we must step back and see the larger picture of Christiandom. Yes, we have a few impressive bonfires burning, but while these flames blaze many of the campfires have gone out. We must see the national picture and turn it around before our grandchildren face the fallout of a leaderless church.

LEADERSHIP DECLINE

In May 2002, while sitting in a dentist office, I picked up the May edition of *Newsweek* magazine to read an article called "Gays and the Seminary." The writer and researcher of this article, David France, wrote that in the year 1965, 49,000 men were entering the priesthood of the Catholic church annually. He went on to say that in 2002 (the year the article was written), fewer than 4,000 men had applied for the priesthood worldwide. He polled the St. Johns Seminary in Camarillo, California, and determined that from 30 percent to 70 percent of the student body entering the priesthood was openly gay, depending on who you asked. This drop in priesthood enrollment, accompanied by the Catholic priest molestation scandals, left them with the worst leadership crisis of their history.

The Protestant world is not much different in raising up new and effective leaders. The *Life Line for Pastors* publication of *Maranatha Life*, in Donna, Texas, they report the following statistics about the crisis of the Protestant pulpits:

⧫ 1,500 pastors leave the ministry each month due to moral failures, spiritual burnout or contention within their church.

⧫ 4,000 new churches begin each year, but 7,000 churches close.

⧫ 50 percent of all pastors' marriages end in divorce.

⧫ 80 percent of all seminary and Bible school graduates who enter the ministry will leave within the first five years.

⧫ 85 percent of pastors say they are sick and tired of dealing with disgruntled leaders.

⧫ 90 percent of pastors say the ministry was completely different from what they thought it would be.

⧫ 80 percent of all pastors' spouses feel their spouse is over worked.

⧫ 70 percent of all pastors do not have a close friend or confidant.

⧫ 85 percent of pastors spend less than 15 minutes a day in prayer.

We have yet another issue that must be addressed. Not only is there a deficit of ministers, but how many of those who enter the ministry are leaders? By leaders, I mean people who are capable of leading denominations or mentoring other ministers in the ever-changing world of the clergy.

THE PARABLE OF THE TREES

Gideon had just died and it was time for his son to take his place as a judge in Israel. Gideon, or Jerubbaal as some nicknamed him after he overthrew the idols of Baal, had left a fearsome legacy. Gideon had 70 sons, but none of them wanted the responsibility of ruling the people of Israel as a judge. Gideon also had a son by a concubine or servant girl who did not have the same honor as a wife, and the boy had not been raised in the atmosphere and influence of the godly Gideon.

When the sons of Gideon decided they did not want to take their place as judge, the men of Israel sought out Abimelech, the renegade son of the servant girl, to be their leader. Abimelech was wreckless, unskilled in leadership and, most of all, lacked anointing. Nevertheless, they still wanted him as the next leader simply because he was a son of a former great leader. In fact, the sons of Gideon got together and paid him 70 shekels of silver to accept the office. He took the money and hired a band of worthless men to come in and kill all 70 sons of Gideon to keep them from changing their minds and taking his place. All of the sons were killed with the exception of Jotham who escaped to proclaim the parable of the trees.

> Now when they told Jotham, he went and stood on top of Mount Gerizim, and lifted his voice and cried out. And he said to them: "Listen to me, you men of Shechem, that God may listen to you! The trees once went forth to anoint a king over them. And they said to the olive tree, 'Reign over us!' But the olive tree said to them, 'Should I cease giving my oil, with which they honor God and men, and go to sway over trees?' Then the trees said to the fig tree, 'You come and reign over us!' But the fig tree said to them, 'Should I cease my sweetness and my good fruit, and go to sway over trees?' Then the trees said to the vine, 'You come and reign over us!' But the vine said to them, 'Should I cease my new wine, which cheers both God and men, and go to sway over trees?' Then all the trees said to the bramble, 'You come and reign over us!' And the bramble said to the trees, 'If in truth you anoint me as king over you, then come and take shelter in my shade; but if not, let fire come out of the bramble and devour the cedars of Lebanon!'" (Judges 9:7-14).

Jotham's parable has a moral: *The only way the wrong man can come into power, is when the right man will not take his rightful place.* He begins by saying the trees wanted a king to rule over them, so they went to the olive tree. The olive tree is the one with the anointing. The olive tree represents those who have truly been anointed to do the work of the Kingdom. The olive tree replied, "Should I cease giving my oil?" In other words, he was comfortable in the anointing he was operating in and did not want to stop what he was doing to lead others. His excuse was his anointing.

Next, they went to the fig tree. The fig tree obviously bears fruit, so it represents someone who is talented and productive, but who still refuses to lead. God has put talent in many people's lives to be used for His kingdom, not to simply build their own little corner of the Kingdom. As in the parable of the talents that Jesus taught, one of these days God will come back and inspect that talent.

> *The only way the wrong man can come into power, is when the right man will not take his rightful place.*

The grapevine was next on their list of preferred leaders. He is the one with the gift of charisma and personality. The vine's excuse was that he would lose his sweetness if he became a leader. He was afraid that he would lose his little cluster of fruit if things changed. He represents a group of people who don't want to lead because they are simply having a good time in their small sphere of influence.

Finally, out of desperation, they went to the bramble. A bramble is a thornbush. The bramble doesn't have anointing, talent or personality. As a matter of fact, he is offensive. He annoyingly sticks and gouges people. He does more to set the Kingdom back than to advance it. He doesn't oper-ate in love, care or compas-sion, but by force and fear. The bramble makes all of them bow down and worship him to prove they are serious about him being their king. He says, "If you are telling the truth, then come here and take shelter under my shade." He is obviously more inter-ested in them serving him than he is in serving them. He threatens to burn them with fire if they refuse.

The called and anointed ones are leaving in groves because they can no longer deal with the pain of disrespectful people.

Unless we can successfully raise up armorbear-ers, we will end up with brambles running our churches. The called and anointed ones are leav-ing in groves because they can no longer deal with the pain of disrespectful people. Remember the Jotham principle:

The only way the wrong man
can come into power,
is when the right man will not
take his rightful place.

DISCUSSION QUESTIONS

1. Discuss why a leaderless army can't march. Do you think many people fail to recognize the absence of genuine leadership?

2. Discuss the potential fallout of ministers leaving the pulpit.

3. Read and discuss the leadership decline statistics.

4. Discuss the parable of the trees.

5. Discuss the last line of the chapter, "The only way the wrong man can come into power is when the right man will not take his rightful place."

When the Philistines were at war again with Israel, David and his servants with him went down and fought against the Philistines; and David grew faint. Then Ishbi-Benob, who was one of the sons of the giant, the weight of whose bronze spear was three hundred shekels, who was bearing a new sword, thought he could kill David. But Abishai the son of Zeruiah came to his aid, and struck the Philistine and killed him. Then the men of David swore to him, saying, "You shall go out no more with us to battle, lest you quench the lamp of Israel" (2 Samuel 21:15-17).

9

Keepers of the Flame

David was a giant-killer (see 1 Samuel 17). As a matter of fact, it was the very gift God used to bring him into his kingship. Can you imagine hearing the people sing their songs about the exploits of David? "David has killed his tens of thousands," they sang. Children would run to meet him in the streets chanting songs of praise after his victories. Standing a head above the rest, he was a national hero—the "giant-killer."

But like every other hero in the world, you soon learn that life moves in seasons, and what was right in one season of your life may not be right in another season. As a matter of fact, one of the most difficult things for leaders to discern is when to let go of something that made them great.

THE BATTLE OF THE GIANTS

The expectations of the crowds can push and pull you in directions away from God's will for a new season and a new harvest of blessings. It was because David killed giants, fought battles, led armies and walked in courage that caused Israel to love and accept their king. He overthrew the Jebusite stronghold and moved his kingdom to "Jebus-salem" (Jerusalem) the ancient city of King Melchizedek. He conquered lands far and wide for his people. All David had to do in order to build national morale was to take his army to war and return home with the spoils. The parades were endless. The people danced in the streets, they feasted for days and experienced prosperity throughout the land. On many occasions he even gave gifts to everyone at the festival. Who would ever want to miss one of King David's parties? All he had to do was keep winning battles.

> All David had to do in order to build national morale was to take his army to war and return home with the spoils.

But while Israel was dancing in the streets season after season, their young king was aging. It became more difficult each time to live up to his notable reputation. The giant-killing, street-dancing, race-running hero was getting older. The day had arrived that David could no longer fight in battles with the strength of his youth. In his younger days, he was saying, "I can run through a troop and leap over a wall" (see 2 Samuel 22:30). Age had changed some of that. In his heart, he could still do all of those things, but in reality, his body would not allow him to leap over walls anymore.

On one particular occasion, while in battle, David came up against one of the sons of the giant. The title alone indicates the large man was much younger than David. However, in typical Davidic fashion, he arrayed himself in warring garments and showed up with the boys. This particular Philistine had one aim in mind: he wanted to be known as the one who killed the giant-killer. His sole purpose that day was to kill David. His name was Ishbi-Benob. He was sporting a new sword and spear and waited for the perfect time to make his move.

The moment arrived. Face-to-face and toe-to-toe, Ishbi-Benob faced the man who had built his reputation killing his relatives. When Ishbi-Benob lunged at the king, who was slightly slower than he used to be, his blow knocked the king of Israel to the ground. The older David was no match for the young, confident giant. The giant stood over the king ready to send the blow that would change the reputation for them both. But Abishai, one of Israel's war champions who happened to be nearby, saw that King David was faint and came to his aid. The king had worn down his opponent, but it was Abishai who had to finish the job. As the day ended, the men of David gathered around him and said, "This is the last time you go to battle with us. We have to keep you alive, or else the lamp of

Israel will go out" (see 2 Samuel 21:17). The younger men were saying, "We can do what you used to do. Right now, we need you to lead us. Let us fight the battles and you lead and train us with your wisdom and years of experience."

A MAN REAPS WHAT HE SOWS

> Let him who is taught the word share in all good things with him who teaches. Do not be deceived, God is not mocked; for whatever a man sows, that he will also reap. For he who sows to his flesh will of the flesh reap corruption, but he who sows to the Spirit will of the Spirit reap everlasting life. And let us not grow weary while doing good, for in due season we shall reap if we do not lose heart. Therefore, as we have opportunity, let us do good to all, especially to those who are of the household of faith (Galatians 6:6-10).

Paul, who never mixed words, writes a straightforward command to the Galatians. This passage is seldom understood or preached in the contextual setting it was presented. Listen closely to the language of the text. "Let him who is taught the word share in all good things with him who teaches" (v. 6).

Paul is literally saying, it is wrong for a person to receive instruction, teaching and guidance from the life of a teacher and not give back to them. It is wrong to take a man or woman's knowledge, resources and life experiences, learn from them, and not give anything back in return.

I have never understood how a person can almost die, go through pain, come out victorious, write it all down in a book and then face complaints from people about having to pay a few dollars for the book. If a person spends years on the battlefield and learns how to defeat the Enemy, it is well worth a few dollars to learn those strategies instead of going into life blindly and learning them for yourself. Too many warriors are wearing out because they are giving more than they are receiving. They are like empty wells that brought life to so many weary travelers, yet no one took the time to pour back into them. Paul says those who receive instruction should share in all good things. He is speaking in particular about the good things that come through the teaching they are receiving.

This means if the teacher gives you the principles to save your house, to walk out of defeat and into prosperity, when you come into your blessing, you should remember his house. If you don't, you are wrong. You have, in fact, taken a man's resources, applied his knowledge, become successful and left him to hurt alone.

It is easy to become empty when everybody is taking from your gift and none of them are giving back from their blessings. It leaves you feeling used up, taken advantage of and lonely. Most ministers do not expect anything in return because they willfully and gladly serve God with their gifts. That is even more reason to bless them. Too many of them come to the end of their days because they can no longer "run through a troop and leap over a wall." They are discarded or demoted instead of being used to teach others what they have learned.

> It is easy to become empty when everybody is taking from your gift and none of them are giving back from their blessings.

GOD IS NOT MOCKED

It is in this very context that we hear the words, "God is not mocked; for whatever a man sows, that he will also reap" (v. 7). In other words, it is not just an injustice to the teacher, it is a mockery to God. The Lord is saying, "I take the time to raise up leaders, call them out, train them, and all I want you to do is take care of them so they can give you what it took Me years to develop in them."

God chooses men and women and places angels around them to teach them. Angels lead these warriors through dark places, rough battles and the school of hard knocks. Others God sends to the classrooms of seminaries where they often have to trust God for every payment, just to finish their education. Many are guided to foreign soil for what they need to be effective ministers. God wrestles with them to deliver them from their pasts, sins and shortcomings. He orders their steps to take them down paths where few have gone and highways where many have never returned.

At the end of this journey of development, God presents our teachers as a gift to His body. He says, "Now learn from your leaders. I have prepared them and gifted them with a special heart, a unique calling and a wealth of experiences so they may be a guiding light in your life. Take care of these men and women so they will not become weary in their work."

God expects us to pour back into our teachers so they can continue to guide and instruct. If we take and do not give, we will eventually be the ones who lose. If you keep reading in Galatians, you will see in verse 9, "And let us not grow weary while doing good, for in due season we shall reap if we do not lose heart."

> If we take and do not give, we will eventually be the ones who lose.

Why should these ministers grow weary while doing good? The answer is that no one is pouring back into their lives. They just keep giving and giving, while no one takes notice of their needs or pains. Too many great teachers have lost heart. Too many have become weary and quit. Too many have given up while doing a good thing.

It is a mockery to take a person's resources and not show gratitude. God says that if you don't understand this principle, you will reap a harvest of corruption in your own life—because if you take and do not give, it is selfish, and selfishness is sin of the flesh. He says that if you then try to sow what you have received selfishly, you will be sowing to the flesh. In turn, you will reap a whirlwind of flesh as your harvest.

God is saying that it is wrong for you to go home with hope in your heart, while your teachers go home and cry themselves to sleep. It is wrong for you to learn how to turn your finances around from a teacher, who then has to struggle to make ends meet. It is wrong for you to receive help saving your marriage while the teacher struggles in his own marriage because no one has taken notice of his weariness. It is wrong for you to grow in the Word while the teacher tires from lack of rest or proper vacations or sabbaticals. It is wrong for you to be healed emotionally while the teacher is discouraged and depressed because everybody takes and no one gives back.

JUST POUR A LITTLE WATER BEFORE YOU LEAVE

A true story is told about a well that was dug in

the middle of the desert. A small hut was built over the well so a weary traveler who was thirsting to death could find it and live. It was miles away from the nearest water. Only desperate people arrived at this desolate place. When a traveler found the hut, there was a jug of water by the hand pump with a note on it. The note said, "If you pour the water from the jug into the pump, this deep well will give you all the water you need, but you must pour the water from the jug in first to prime the pump. When you leave, be sure and fill the jug up again or the next traveler will not be able to get any water from the well."

Each desperate person had to make a decision whether to drink the water in the jug, or to take the risk of pouring it down the old hand pump in order to prime it. Each time they poured the water out by faith, they knew if the old well was dry, they would die in the desert of thirst. But the fact that the jug still had water in it gave them hope that someone had traveled that way before and left water in the jug. Once the water was poured out by faith into the pump, they would desperately start pumping the handle and soon, as much water as they could drink would come gushing out. They had enough water to wash, fill their canteens and drink their fill. But they had to be responsible enough to remember to fill the jug before leaving so the next traveler could get to the water. If only one of them refused to fill the jug, the water would be lost from that time on.

So many teachers are like that old well. All they need is a little in order to give a lot. We have to remember that when our lives are saved from their water that was filled with hope and instructions, we need to take time to fill the jug before we leave. If we do not give back, soon another weary traveler will come to that same well, but the pump will be dry. There will be nothing wrong with the water—it is still there—but there is no way to get to it because the pump has dried out.

KEEPERS OF THE FLAME

> Their duty included the ark, the table, the lampstand, the altars, the utensils of the sanctuary with which they ministered, the screen, and all the work relating to them. And Eleazar the son of Aaron the priest was to be chief over the leaders of the Levites, with oversight of those who kept charge of the sanctuary (Numbers 3:31, 32).

Go with me in your imagination to the Tabernacle of Moses erected in the wilderness wanderings of Israel. I want you to see a typical day for the Levites. Their job was to keep the Tabernacle and ordinances of God operating at all times. Each Levite had specific instructions. Some gathered and carried wood for the altar. Some attended to the water in the laver. Some baked and changed out the bread in the Holy Place. Others washed the garments of the priests.

Many were assigned to sing, play musical instruments and fill the atmosphere with praise. One of the Levitical duties was to make sure the light of the candlestick never went out. It had to burn continuously day and night. It was the symbol of Christ and the Holy Spirit in the Tabernacle. In order to fulfill this responsibility, they had to keep fresh oil and wicks nearby at all times.

A few years ago, I preached a series of sermons on "The Tabernacle of Moses." I broke down each symbol and piece of furniture to its primary function, as well as its symbolic meaning. When I got to the candlestick, it was easy to see that it was a symbol of Christ. The candlestick was made in appearance like an almond tree. Its branches had knobs, buds and flowers on each stem modeled after an almond branch in the spring of the year.

The Hebrew word for *almond* means "awakening," which is an allusion to the almond blossom, which is first to bloom in the spring. The almond's pinkish-white blossoms always appear before its leaves. The awakening of Jeremiah's ministry started with an almond branch (see Jeremiah 1:11, 12). The rod of Aaron that budded was an almond branch; Jeremiah's and Zechariah's "righteous Branch" was an almond branch. The trunk of the candlestick (or lampstand) symbolized the righteous Branch (the Messiah) and the first to bloom in the spring, which spoke of Jesus and the Resurrection. It also had six other branches.

In prophetic Scripture, *six* is the number of man. This too speaks of us being engrafted into the true Vine, which is Christ. The bowls at the top of each candlestick were shaped like almonds. They symbolized the fruit of the tree, or the fruit of the Spirit as it relates to the life of the believer.

There is an interesting principle that must not be overlooked in this spiritual analogy. The fire can only come out of the fruit, not the fruit out of the fire. The anointing of God comes through lives that bear fruit, not gifts. God said over and over to His people, "Be fruitful and multiply." We can never rely solely on our gifts to bring God's anointing. It is the fruit of our lives He desires.

> The anointing of God comes through lives that bear fruit, not gifts.

The fire and the oil in the bowls represent the work of the Holy Spirit. But, the fire can only burn if it has a wick. The wick had to be trimmed daily by the priests, according to Exodus 27:21. It is that daily trimming that catches my attention. This majestic golden candlestick, with its pristine pure oil and its brilliant flame depends on a tiny wick in order to give its light. The brilliance of the room is lost if the wick is not trimmed.

The radiance of this Holy Place is never seen if the

wick is not trimmed. The table of bread is never dis-
covered. This tiny free-floating wick, while barely noticed because of the flame, is absolutely key to keeping the Holy Place alive and lit. This wick, among virgin oil and pure gold, is the only element of imperfection in this entire scene, yet it is absolutely necessary. The wick is the natural conduit needed to get the oil and flame to the room. The wick can wear out, wear down and even burn out. That is why it is necessary to trim it every day so the lamp will not go out.

> We need men and women who will take it upon themselves to be keepers of the flame.

This wick is the minister. It is the imperfect path to which God transfers the supernatural into the atmosphere of the natural. It is the vulnerable small conduit of transferred anointing. This tiny oil-soaked piece of straw and cotton allows the oil to get to the flame, and the flame to get to the darkness.

We need men and women who will take it upon themselves to be keepers of the flame. Oh that God would raise up wick trimmers, oil pourers and fire lighters so that the wicks God has chosen to be His spiritual conduit can keep the flame burning.

DISCUSSION QUESTIONS

1. Discuss the process of a leader's life.

    a. What are some things a leader should have to deal with on one level that he or she didn't have to do on a previous level?

    b. What are some things a seasoned man should no longer be required to do that a novice was expected to do while earning his stripes?

2. Discuss the five giants David and his men killed. Could this be the reason David collected five stones in the beginning?

3. Read the Galatians 6:6-10 passage on communication in all good things, and discuss this with the person who is teaching you.

4. Discuss the law of sowing and reaping.

5. Discuss the concept of becoming weary in well doing.

Now Amalek came and fought with Israel in Rephidim. And Moses said to Joshua, "Choose us some men and go out, fight with Amalek. Tomorrow I will stand on the top of the hill with the rod of God in my hand." So Joshua did as Moses said to him, and fought with Amalek. And Moses, Aaron, and Hur went up to the top of the hill. And so it was, when Moses held up his hand, that Israel prevailed; and when he let down his hand, Amalek prevailed. But Moses' hands became heavy; so they took a stone and put it under him, and he sat on it. And Aaron and Hur supported his hands, one on one side, and the other on the other side; and his hands were steady until the going down of the sun. So Joshua defeated Amalek and his people with the edge of the sword (Exodus 17:8-13).

10

Hands On, Hands Up and Hands Under

One of the most difficult tasks for a leader is to let go. When a ministry begins, the leader starts out "with the people." As a fisher of men, he or she starts out fishing with a fishing rod—catching them one by one. The leader is usually the one who leads them to the Lord, disciples them, cares for them, trains them and gives them their first Kingdom assignment.

GOING BEFORE THE PEOPLE

At this stage, the fellowship and friendships are within the congregation. As the leader, you become everyone's buddy and together all of you create a community of faith and friendship. The "with-the-people" relationship can be rewarding, but like all intimate relationships where people know your business, it can also be painful.

One of the tragedies of leadership is that you can begin to get possessive of the things God asks you to manage. God is always the landlord of Kingdom property. When you start feeling possessive, it becomes difficult to let go and release people into their own ministry or another field of labor where God decides to send them. The "with-the-people" ministry, while socially rewarding, is also limited. You can only be friends with a certain number of people at a time.

In order for God to allow the leadership and the people to grow spiritually, God had to send Moses and the elders of Israel, "before the people."

> And the Lord said to Moses, "Go on before the people, and take with you some of the elders of Israel. Also take in your hand your rod with which you struck the river, and go" (v. 5).

The people were complaining and murmuring against Moses. They became too familiar with him and the other leaders. Familiarity often breeds con-

If you want to know if you are leading, look behind you and see if anyone is following.

tempt. But when God moves them beyond the people, they are able to separate themselves from the common concerns and focus on the big picture. Not only that, but now they are also able to fellowship more with God and hear His voice more clearly.

This began to produce miracles in the midst of Israel, and with the new level of leadership came a new level of anointing. Water was now flowing from a rock and everyone's thirst was being quenched. It is almost impossible to lead when you are walking with the crowd. You can't lead from the back, you can only lead from the front. If you want to know if you are leading, look behind you and see if anyone is following. If they are, you are a leader; if they are not, you are only taking a walk. "Going before the people" released Moses from the day-to-day cares of life and murmurings of the people. With a clear mind and heart, he could now speak the words of the Lord to the people.

GOING ABOVE THE PEOPLE

Leadership alone will not cause a church to grow. I'm not talking about the leadership of one man or woman. I am referring to the ability to raise up many leaders within the congregation. After a while, the leadership will grow to the point that you have to separate yourself again in order to take the church to the next level. It is in the "high places" with God that you will find the greatest anointing of your ministry. This is the third dimension of leadership. Level one is "with the people." Level two is going "before the people." Level three is when God calls you "above the people."

"Above the people" does not refer to social status. It does not mean that you are better than the people; it means that God is establishing order within the congregation and you have to go to the high place spiritually in order to lead your diverse and growing group. However, one issue that faces the leader whom God calls to "go up" is loneliness. At this level, you deal with feeling out of control because you can't touch the lives of the people you lead anymore.

One of the things Moses had to do was send down someone he trusted to fight "with the people." He could only use someone whose trust had been with him through all three levels. He chose Joshua—someone he knew was loyal to him. He also needed someone who didn't need him to help solve all of the problems. He knew Joshua could fight without worrying Moses about the details. Moses did not need to solve problems of that type anymore at his level. He needed someone who could handle the battle without someone holding his hand.

HANDS ON AND HANDS UP

Moses had to have a Joshua to have his "hands on" in order to go to the spiritual level to have his "hands up." You cannot have your hands up and have hands on at the same time. You will never be able to go to the spiritual levels you need to unless you can let go of the hands-on experience.

Hands-on ministries are

> You cannot have your hands up and have hands on at the same time.

intimate and socially fulfilling, but they are limited. On every level of ministry, you have to separate more and more from your people. In Jesus' ministry, He started out teaching thousands. He chose 12 to lead, but He only chose three to go to the intimate places with Him.

As you begin to go higher, you can only go with people you trust with your life. Trouble will come to your leadership system when you move someone from level one to level two or three when they don't belong there. Everybody can't go up. Everybody can't be in the inner circle. When you bring someone in your inner circle that does not have your backing, you are asking for trouble.

Some people need to stay in the outer circle.

> The higher place of church leadership is the place where spiritual warfare is fought and won.

- ♦ Those in the outer circle love you for your gift, but they really don't know you.

- ♦ Those who are in the middle circle will serve you, but will turn on you as soon as you offend them.

- ♦ Those who can go up with you are those who serve you and stay with you no matter what.

Elijah gave Elisha several opportunities to leave, but he failed to do so. He earned the right to be in the inner circle because of his commitment to the prophet.

You can only go higher when you find people who will keep their hands under your tired arms. The higher place of church leadership is the place where spiritual warfare is fought and won. It is the place where you tear down strongholds and kill spiritual giants—the place where you conquer and work in a rare dimension that few ever reach. The leader who goes up enters that realm with a dilemma.

First of all, the people you serve want your gift, but do not always want you. Secondly, your middle management leadership wants to be with you all the time because that is where they have been used to operating. When you go up, they are still before the people, but now you have had to separate from them also. They miss you and you miss them, but in order for you to help them go free, you must move into the realm of things over their heads and have a face-off with principalities and rulers of darkness. So when you enter the third dimension of leadership, you go there with a heavier spiritual load, but with the smallest support system you have operated with in years.

HANDS UNDER

The inner circle of Moses' life was entrusted to

his older brother, Aaron, and his brother-in-law, Hur. The historian Josephus says that Hur was the husband of Moses' sister, Miriam. These were the two people he trusted the most.

Joshua knew how to fight "with the people." He was the "hands-on" leader. The elders of Israel knew how to lead "before the people." They became the "hands-up" leaders. Remember that Moses took them to the mountain of God to meet with God.

The group became firmly established with spiritual leadership—the operational side, run by Joshua, and the spiritual side, run by Aaron and the elders, were now in position. It was time to conquer and defeat the enemies.

The scene took place in a valley. This is certainly symbolic of the places we live, but more so of the places we fight. The army gathered and Joshua prepared to fight.

There is only so much an army can do. "For we do not wrestle against flesh and blood, but against principalities, against powers, against the rulers of the darkness of this age, against spiritual hosts of wickedness in the heavenly places" (Ephesians 6:12). The elders stayed back with the women and children while the army went to battle. I am sure they were interceding and praying and giving comfort and assurance to those who had family in the battle.

Moses took his position at the top of the mountain with his stick. The stick he carried was a tangible symbol God gave him to represent His power. It was the stick that consumed the sorcery of Pharaoh's wizards, the stick that called down the plagues of Egypt, the stick that parted the waters at the Red Sea, and the stick God used to bring the miracles in the wilderness.

He had his stick and his position with God, but all of that was not enough. The long battle was tiring. As long as his hands were up, Israel prevailed, but when he got tired and his hands dropped, the enemy began to win the battle.

His two trusted confidants, his inner-circle people, saw what was going on and rushed to his side. As a great leader, you can't let just anyone see your vulnerabilities. You can be transparent, but not weak. Transparent communication allows the people to relate to you, but those same people should not be in on your personal struggles.

> Transparent communication allows the people to relate to you, but those same people should not be in on your personal struggles.

These two men, who loved and trusted Moses, held up his arms during the battle. The battle against the Amalekites was not won because of Joshua. As good as he was, they would have been defeated that day if it was left only to his abilities. It was not even won because of Moses. Moses was great and his stick was with him, but his flesh was too weak for such a long battle. The battle against the Amalekites was won that day because of Aaron and Hur. Without them being in their places to lift up the hands of this great leader, the battle would have been lost.

"Hands on" can only get you to the first level of leadership and victory. "Hands up" can take you higher, and can set the people free. But the only way to put the Enemy to flight and take charge of the spiritual atmosphere within your sphere of assignment is to have "hands-under" ministers in place who make sure you do not quit too early, you don't wear out too quickly, and you don't become weary in well-doing.

Thank God for armorbearers!

DISCUSSION QUESTIONS

1. Discuss the title of this chapter and its meaning.

2. Put the concept "before the people" into a practical situation everyone can identify with and discuss (perhaps the role of their pastor or leader).

3. Do the same thing with the concept of "above the people." Discuss the resistance of the crowd to allow a leader to go up in order to lead.

4. Discuss the characters of Aaron and Hur. What type of men do you think they were and why did they go up with Moses instead of someone else?

5. Discuss the inner circle of a leader's life. How many people do you think can be in that inner circle, and what determines who can become a part of the group that has its ear and undivided attention?

When the Son of Man comes in His glory, and all the holy angels with Him, then He will sit on the throne of His glory. All the nations will be gathered before Him, and He will separate them one from another, as a shepherd divides his sheep from the goats. And He will set the sheep on His right hand, but the goats on the left. Then the King will say to those on His right hand, "Come, you blessed of My Father, inherit the kingdom prepared for you from the foundation of the world: for I was hungry and you gave Me food; I was thirsty and you gave Me drink; I was a stranger and you took Me in; I was naked and you clothed Me; I was sick and you visited Me; I was in prison and you came to Me." Then the righteous will answer Him, saying, "Lord, when did we see You hungry and feed You, or thirsty and give You drink? When did we see You a stranger and take You in, or naked and clothe You? Or when did we see You sick, or in prison, and come to You?" And the King will answer and say to them, "Assuredly, I say to you, inasmuch as you did it to one of the least of these My brethren, you did it to Me" (Matthew 25:31-40).

11

Portraits of Armorbearers

In the United States Military, chaplains are not allowed to carry a weapon. Instead, each chaplain is assigned a body guard when on the battlefield or in a place of danger.

I want you to imagine this scene for a moment. There is smoke all around. The sounds of war are deafening. It is almost impossible to see or hear. You can hear the cries of the wounded, the whistling of missiles in the air, the buzz of bullets flying around you. It's overwhelming, to say the least. All you can think of is finishing the mission and going home. Each warrior is armed and dangerous. Each has a weapon and other artillery designed to engage the enemy and protect his or her own life.

Yet, in this place of bravery, there is a group that stands tall in their private and unsung world of heroism. This elite group is known as military chaplains. They are on the same battlefield, and their only weapon is their faith. Many of them die while serving the men and women who are ready and desperate to call on the name of God in their hour of danger. They baptize converts in trenches and hold services in the open air or in tents. Military chaplains serve sacraments, give counsel, carry the wounded, and comfort the dying with a Bible in their hand, but no weapon at their side. This brave lot can be found everywhere there are soldiers. Chaplains are on the ships, in the tankers, aboard the planes and in the trenches with the fighting forces. They answer the call of every national and international crisis. You will find chaplains among the fighting forces, on the disaster relief teams and literally anywhere their services are needed.

One of the reasons they can be so brave is because each of them is assigned an armorbearer. That is not his title, but that is certainly his assignment. The job of these armorbearers is to go into the combat zone with the chaplains and protect their lives while they minister. The armorbearers stand in front of the chaplains and lead them to places of safety. They stand behind the chaplains while they lean over a dying soldier who is within minutes of death. They cover chaplains many times while they carry the wounded to a place of safety. While others are fighting the enemy, these lone soldiers are protecting the chaplains with their own lives.

> Military chaplains serve sacraments, give counsel, carry the wounded, and comfort the dying with a Bible in their hand, but no weapon at their side.

The duality of this team is what makes it work. Chaplains would not be able to perform their duties without the aid of the brave armorbearers who watch their backs. This amazing portrait of protection gives a vivid and life-related picture of one who protects another so they may give their best. Many of these brave ones will receive a medal of honor while in this life. But in the other realm of reality, the heavenly realm, another reward awaits them—a crown of glory that does not fade away.

WIND TALKERS

In World War II, the nations of the world battled with their allies to stop the Nazi regime and its hellish ideas. Technology was just beginning to advance, and this war saw air strikes and newly invented artillery of war for the first time. It seemed as

> Chaplains would not be able to perform their duties without the aid of the brave armorbearers who watch their backs.

though the sides were well matched. The onslaught of killing and devastation continued to claim lives in a series of bloody battles.

War is always ugly and this one was no different. One of the problems encountered by the U.S. armed forces was the fact that the enemy kept breaking their codes, making it impossible to penetrate their forces enough to turn the tide of the war. Needing a new resource, they found it in the heart of the Navajo Indian nation.

The Navajo Indians had been repressed by the white man for many years. They had been run off their land and stripped of their pride and resources. However, with the threat of war nearing U.S. soil, the Navajo decided to put aside their grievances and pull together in order to protect their homeland.

The Navajo had a gift that was needed in this battle—a complicated language made up of voice inflections that, when altered, changed the meaning of the word or phrase. The Navajo language still holds the title of being the most difficult language in the world to master. Listening to the Navajo communicate sounds almost like a series of grunts and moans.

The U.S. military employed Navajo Indians during this war to send instructions and locator messages for the military. The enemy did not know what to do with this language. Their native tongue was better than any code used before. The enemy was baffled and the tide of war turned to our favor, because of these brave Navajo Indians. People who heard the Navajo speak this language began to call them Wind Talkers.

Since the war depended on radio operators to send and receive the orders or give the position of the enemy, the safety of each Navajo was of utmost importance. The Navajo were given a personal body guard to keep them alive in battle. The bravery of these armorbearers was just as important as the bravery of the Wind Talkers. Each man had to fulfill his role in order to win the battle.

This war was won primarily because of this new communication tool. However, their messages could never have been delivered without the fearlessness of the people who kept them alive. They pulled the Wind Talkers from foxhole to foxhole. The untold stories of the armorbearers who sacrificed their own lives for the sake of the cause are countless. Many of these men had to lay aside their own preconceived prejudices in order to serve honorably. This is an incredible picture of people who lay aside their personal agendas to serve a bigger cause in life.

> The Navajo were given a personal body guard to keep them alive in battle. The bravery of these armorbearers was just as important as the bravery of the Wind Talkers.

MILITARY MEDICS

It seems like armorbearers do their best work in places where others do not want to serve. They don't always serve in dangerous places, but they serve people whose presence is vital to the success of a plan, purpose or organization.

In this chapter we have dealt primarily with war scenes. I like these portraits because they depict people who are willing to put their lives on the line to serve another. While these illustrations may seem extreme, they are real-life situations that illustrate the character and bravery of those who serve.

Another brave group that can be found in the gravest of situations is military medics. They work under the most extreme and adverse conditions, performing surgeries in an instant, under conditions that are deplorable. They risk their own lives in each enemy engagement. The troops in combat are in the business of taking the lives of the enemy while the medics work tirelessly to save the lives of the troops.

While the medics risk their own lives to save others, another risks his or her life to protect the life of the medic.

Without any regard for their own safety, the medics go where the danger is, because that is precisely where their patients are. Many of them have lost their own lives in order to save the lives of others. Medics work in dirty, bloody, smoky, dangerous places in order to bring others home from war.

These conditions are unique because they portray a lifesaver protecting another lifesaver. While the medics risk their own lives to save others, another risks his or her life to protect the life of the medic. This reminds me of the story in Nehemiah 4 where part of the men worked to build the wall, while another group protected them from the enemy with spears and bows. The work of the craftsman hinged upon the ability of the armorbearer to protect him while he worked.

WHEN THE GOING GETS TOUGH, THE TOUGH GET GOING

The walls of heaven must be lined with the trophies and medals awaiting these selfless servants. Their secret sacrifices have not gone unrecorded in the courts of heaven. I am certain that celestial beings sing their heroic anthems. "By and by when the morning comes and all the saints have gathered home," I believe we will hear songs written by angels to commemorate and declare the eternal glory and honor of those who served silently and selflessly.

Perhaps this is why the Lord said the first will be last and the last will be first (Matthew 19:30). If heaven has a parade, I believe armorbearers will wave from the streets as people line the grandstands to commemorate their lives.

Armorbearers are not people who can't do anything but serve. On the contrary, they are the toughest of the tough. They are the bravest of the brave.

Their servanthood comes at a great cost. They have overcome jealousy, pride, victim-thinking and selfishness to take up their crosses and follow Christ. This elite group has known nothing but private victories, for the honor went to the ones they served. Their coronation still awaits them. I can't wait to see their crowns, hear their new names and, most of all, hear Him say, "Well done . . . enter into the joys of the Lord."

> Armorbearers
> are not
> people who
> can't do
> anything
> but serve.

DISCUSSION QUESTIONS

1. Discuss the story of the military chaplain's armorbearer. See if anyone in the group has witnessed this scene firsthand.

2. Discuss the story of the Wind Talkers. Especially discuss the prejudices that existed during that time and emotional issues that each military armorbearer had to overcome in order to do his job well.

3. Discuss the story of the military medics. See if anyone in the group has a related story.

4. Discuss the heavenly reward of armorbearers. What types of honors do you think will be bestowed upon this elite group of servants?

5. Discuss the tough nature of an armorbearer. What type of character flaws or hindrances do you think would keep a person from fulfilling this role?

6. What type of character traits do you think would make the ideal armorbearer?

7. Discuss roles of people in the kingdom of God who need armorbearers.

THE ARMORBEARER'S PLEDGE

I am a part of God's strategic secret force, for I serve in His army of armorbearers.

✦

I will not give up in the face of adversity, for I have been anointed to bring God's champions back from battle.

✦

I will not give in to negative conversation, for I fight at the back of the one God has assigned to me for preservation.

✦

I will not feel sorry for myself when my efforts go unnoticed, because my reward will come at the end of the battle, when the King crowns me for my valor.

✦

I will not sit on the sidelines of the battle of life while my officer wears out, for I have been given the assignment to pour water over his hands and keep him refreshed.

✦

I will not forget to cover my officer in prayer, for prayer is how I suit him up with the armor of God for that day.

✦

I will not forget to check on the well-being of my officer, for God has entrusted him to my care.

✦

I will not forget to fill his life with words of encouragement, hugs and tokens of my care and affection, for I am a keeper of the flame.

✦

I will not forget to celebrate the members of their family to insure victories in his private world.

✦

I can and will fulfill this divine assignment because I am ... confident in my calling, secure in my position, anointed in my service, and prepared for the challenge!

✦

I am prayed up, fired up and, every day, I am sharpening up until the day I go up to meet the One who filled me up and called me up to the higher ground I now walk on.

✦

I will be the wind beneath the wings of the champion. I will be the one hiding in the shadows to make sure my officer shines. I will be the one who does everything necessary to make sure my officer can lead the troops to victory. I do not care if anyone recognizes me or knows my name as long as God knows who I am, where I am and that I am doing what He called me to do.

✦

I am not afraid of ridicule nor ashamed of giving my glory to another, for one day I will stand before my Lord and King to receive my just reward. My due season is "to do whatever it takes" to keep God's champions in the battle and to keep the enemy on the run. I will fight to the finish and no one will get to my officer unless they go through me, for I am a part of the elite fighting force of God's armorbearers.